One Coast To Another

Following Wainwright from St Bees to Robin Hood's Bay

Andrew Bowden

Text and photographs
©2010, 2014, 2015 Andrew Paul Bowden
All rights reserved

The right of Andrew Bowden to be identified as the Author of the work has been asserted by him in accordance with the Copyright, Designs and Patents Act 1998.

First published, 2010 by Rambling Man Books
Second paperback edition published 2015

ISBN   1508870934
ISBN-13   978-1508870937

For Catherine

Contents

Introduction..7
Day 1 - St Bees to Ennerdale Bridge.......................11
Day 2 - Ennerdale Bridge to Borrowdale...............21
Day 3 - Borrowdale to Patterdale..........................31
Day 4 - Patterdale to Bampton..............................41
Day 5 - Bampton to Orton......................................51
Day 6 - Orton to Kirkby Stephen...........................59
Day 7 - Kirkby Stephen to Keld.............................67
Day 8 - Keld to Reeth...75
Day 9 - Reeth to Brompton-on-Swale via Richmond
....83
Day 10 - Brompton-on-Swale to Ingleby Cross.....93
Day 11 - Ingleby Cross to Clay Bank Top.............103
Day 12 - Clay Bank Top to Blakey Ridge..............111
Day 13 - Blakey Ridge to Grosmont......................119
Day 14 - Grosmont to Robin Hood's Bay.............131
About The Author...139
Planning Your Own Trip Walking the Coast to Coast..141
Discover other books by Andrew Bowden..........154
Connect with Andrew Bowden............................155

Cumbria in Bloom-Winners
Britain in Bloom-Finalists
ST. BEES
Start of
Coast-to-Coast
Walk

Introduction

There are ways to begin a long distance walk. Things that must be done. It's compulsory. It's written in the rules.

First you must stride purposefully to the starting point. You must fill your lungs with a deep breath. You must have a photograph taken next to the sign, monument or obelisk that marks the beginning of the trail. And you must proclaim loudly and clearly to all who will listen: "And so it begins!"

Of course it's best to do all that whilst there is no one else watching. And preferably whilst not wearing waterproof trousers that are three sizes too small for you.

I scored a win on the first one....

It had all started so well. The day before we'd set off from Lancaster on a packed one carriage train plodding along the Cumbrian coastline. Catherine had bagged a prime spot at a table in the middle of the carriage and on the left hand side, meaning we'd get a great view (meanwhile I'd been getting the teas in - well a two hour train journey with no buffet facility? You just have to....) despite being on a hopelessly overcrowded train.

"It's always two carriages this train in the winter, yet as soon as the tourists turn up, they take one off!" declared one local woman on her way back home with shopping bags groaning on the luggage rack above her head, whilst we were busy admiring the view of the Irish Sea.

It was as if she thought there was some mad maniac at the heart of Northern Rail cackling "Tourists? Tourists! I'll make them suffer.... SUFFER YOU HEAR ME!". Although that said.... just where exactly did the other carriage go?

At Barrow-in-Furness the packed train almost completely emptied before instantly refilling with commuters heading home. Then we passed Sellafield - that mighty palace to nuclear energy - and before we knew it, we were at our destination. The small, unassuming village of St Bees.

But St Bees holds a special place in the heart of the true long distance walker, for it is the place that one Alfred Wainwright decided to start what is perhaps his masterpiece: "A Coast To Coast Walk".

A walk of nearly two hundred miles across the north of England from St Bees on the west, through Cumbria and North Yorkshire all the way to Robin Hood's Bay on the eastern coast.

It was a walk Catherine had always wanted to do. So we decided to do it. We planned our itinerary to split it over 14 days, booked accommodation and waited, oh how we waited, for the off.

And now it was here. Soon we'd be setting off. Soon we'd be on our way. We'd arrived, had a good night's sleep and were ready to begin.

There was just one problem. It had been raining all night, and was still going as we got ready to set off. We dutifully prepared to don our waterproofs in our B&B room when disaster struck.

My nice, shiny new(ish) breathable waterproof trousers seemed to have gone AWOL, replaced instead by an old, redundant, non-breathable and rather small pair of Catherine's.

Left with no option but to squeeze in, I walked the mile and a half from our B&B to the beach, the tightness of the trousers frankly leaving very little to the imagination....

NO
PIES
BREAD &
MILK
PAPERS
POTATOES
FRUIT & VEG
DRINKS
SANDWICHES

Day 1 - St Bees to Ennerdale Bridge

"And so it begins"

In walking circles Alfred Wainwright is a legend. His little pictorial guides are truly treasured by all who go walking in his favoured "Lakeland" - now more commonly known as the Lake District.

Wainwright never seemed happier than when he was out on the fells and in the late 1960s he set off to catalogue what was perhaps the best known walking route in Britain - the newly created Pennine Way.

To say Wainwright hated it may be an understatement. He found it a serious trudge. So much was his despair at the thing that he decided that anyone completing it in full deserved a pint. On him. Until he died he paid the bills at the Border Hotel in Kirk Yetholm, and although his money has long run out, the tradition is maintained by brewing giant Greene King who provide Morland Original for the purposes, although in the slightly smaller half pint size.

Wainwright took it upon himself to create a more pleasing walk. A walk where the intention was about enjoyment, interest and variety rather than merely following some geographical feature like most national trails.

Detailed in his book, *A Coast to Coast Walk*, it has become one of the most popular walking routes in Britain. An estimated 9,000 people set off on it every year. Scores of books are written, and plenty of maps sold. Many villages en-route benefit hugely from the walkers that pass through.

Yet the Coast to Coast has no legal status and very limited signage. It just is, and remains "just is" over its 190 odd mile length.

It was this legal non-entity that we were about to set off on - extremely tight waterproof trousers and all (what you do you mean you skipped the introduction?)

* * *

Our B&B landlady thought we were mad, but that was mainly because we turned down her kind offer of a lift to the village. We'd had trouble booking anywhere in St Bees to stay, and the only bed we'd found had been at Moorclose B&B, a mile up a steep road out of St Bees proper. But we thought there was little point; we'd come here to walk and what difference did a mile and a half extra make?

Down in the village we stocked up on supplies in the local store, passed the Queens Hotel we'd frequented the night before, and headed for the sea.

There's two traditions associated with the Coast to Coast. Firstly Wainwright encouraged everyone to dip their boots into the Irish Sea before setting off, and again in the North Sea at the end.

And then there's the pebble. You pick one up at the start and leave it at the beach at the end. It's a tradition which frankly gave me images of fleets of lorries carting stones back across the country to fill the gap left at Robin Hood's Bay.

Our pebbles dutifully chosen, our boots suitably soggy, we headed for the hills but not before I gave up and decided rain or no, wearing waterproof trousers three sizes too small was not good. But then it had stopped raining anyway.

The Coast to Coast starts in style, rising high up on the cliffs and walking around them towards Whitehaven, providing amazing views on a good day, which thankfully it was. In part.

Whilst the rain had gone, the wind that had howled around our B&B the night before, had remained and was doing a sterling job of trying to blow us to the floor.

The waves crashed into the rocks below as we came along the headland, past St Bees lighthouse, with Ireland, the Isle of Man, Scotland and more just visible in the cloudy distance.

Passing by a quarry (with some portable toilets provided by the amusingly named "Borderloos") we headed inland, passing a boat with a bizarre mannequin dressed in a sow-wester, and a huge St Bernard dog parked on a wall who resisted any attempt to stroke him by gently batting my arm down with his paw so that he could lick the sweat off it.

From here on it was relatively flat walking, skirting the sights of Whitehaven in the near distance to pass down into the village of Sandwith.

Away from the coastal wind, things were hotting up and we took the opportunity to park ourselves on a handy bench and strip off layers of clothes, adjust our boots and re-apply the inevitable factor 50.

From there on we passed alongside fields and walked down lanes before going under a railway line and into a soggy field swelled by heavy rain a few days earlier.

Our route now seemed to take us along a wooded, sheltered road; the kind that looks like no one has used in years. The kind adventurers find themselves on whilst on a quest. The kind where epics are born.

And maybe they were. But if they were, well we sure weren't supposed to know.

We'd gone the wrong way. A sign next to the gate told us so, complete with directions of how to get back on track. Whilst a useful, thoughtful measure - and a mistake no doubt many made if someone had gone to the trouble of putting up a makeshift poster - notice a little earlier might just have been a little more useful!

It wasn't a huge detour and we quickly joined the cycle path that now runs along the dismantled Egremont Extension railway, which provides an alternative to Wainwright's original route (and wild raspberries - yum!) along the roads and village of Moor Row before gently depositing the walker near a sewage works in Cleator.

Cleator is perhaps best known for its red

sandstone church, but for us it will be forever known for its sign outside advertising the fact that the shop sold bread and milk, papers, potatoes, fruit and veg, drinks and sandwiches. Then at the top, in big bold letters, it proudly proclaimed "NO PIES".

Clearly it's a place where you can get your bread, your milk, your papers, your potatoes, your fruit and your veg (cos potatoes aren't veg). You can get your drinks and your sandwiches too. But not your pies. No. For there are no pies. No. None at all.

Clearly lack of pies is a big thing in Cleator. Why, I can't say. Are they truly amazing pies? Do people come from miles around to buy their pies from there? Either way lack of pies is clearly such a big deal that they have an interchangeable sign outside informing you of pie status, so that instead of going in to the shop and finding there be no pies, you can find out on the street and be disappointed there instead.

These must be amazing pies. But I wouldn't know. Because there were none.

* * *

Cleator now gave way to the main, and indeed only challenge of the day: Dent Fell.

Its lower slopes are forested and a steep but firm logging road zig-zags its way up to just before the top, where the Coast to Coast walker must turn off to get to the sheep grazed summit.

The reward for your effort is most gratifying

with a huge cairn to celebrate the achievement, and a stunning view to boot. An amazing panorama was revealed: Whitehaven, St Bees, Sellafield, Scotland and Ireland on one side, and a fine introduction to the Lake District on the other.

Views were not all that we were treated to. As we stopped to say hello to two women resting on the hillside, they invited us to stop a minute and listen.

"It's either bagpipes of an ice cream van" proclaimed one.

"Well I would prefer the ice cream van - I could murder a 99!" extolled the other, and with that, who could disagree.

"There's a man who plays, fully dressed in the full kit up around the border" she continued, however further playing drifting through the hills we did not hear. Almost as if the player knew they had an audience, the pipes stopped a playin'. Normality - the sounds of birds tweeting and the wind blowing - was restored.

Such rewards of great views and live music almost inevitably come at a price and the descent downhill was a serious one. Incredibly steep, it was the kind of hill that a hiker with a full pack on their back dreads, especially on the first day. We were carrying everything on our backs and the weight really distorts your centre of balance. Bending down too much has the potential to see you go off tumbling down the hill before finally getting to the bottom dizzy, dusty and, most likely, in a big crumpled ball.

The cartoon style birds circling our heads

thankfully never came, but it was a relief to get to the bottom of the valley and walk the four or so flat miles to Ennerdale Bridge where we'd be staying for the night.

By now we'd caught up with a plethora of other walkers and following the crowd we almost missed the Kinniside stone circle. There are many such circles on the Coast to Coast and this must be the finest and best looking, although there's a good reason for that - unlike its ancient brethren, it's actually a relatively modern re-creation built by an archaeologist. Still, its power was still felt. By someone. Somewhere....

Ennerdale Bridge was now in sight and we headed into the village, passing its two pubs and knocked on the door to our B&B before heading out again for food and an enchanting night at the Shepherd's Arms Hotel. Despite it being a Friday night it seemed to be catering solely for walkers. Not one local person darkened its doors for a pint of Ennerdale Copper or a bite to eat. But then given they microwaved a homemade steak and ale pie with suet pastry - a major travesty - perhaps they all knew better.

Maybe it was the microwaved pastry. Maybe because the landlord had alienated all the villagers... Well who knows. If you're thinking the second pub might have been better - well let us just say the same person runs it. Maybe it was busier. Who knew? Either way by half eight on a Friday night the place consisted of two customers and a woman behind the bar. Doing my bit for the rather depressing local economy, I ordered another pint.

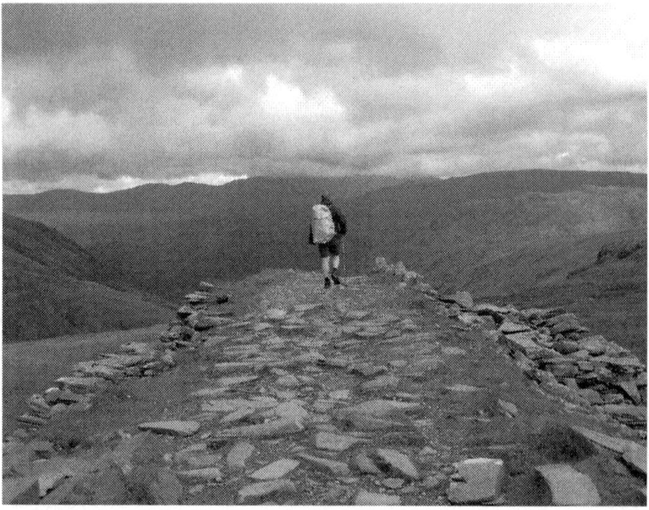

Day 2 - Ennerdale Bridge to Borrowdale

"Eeeee, welcome t'mine...."

A few weeks before we were due to set off walking on the Coast to Coast, Britain was in the midst of a major league heatwave.

Newspaper headlines screamed about "scorchers" and hosepipe bans, whilst middle aged men in suits and ties dabbed their foreheads with handkerchiefs.

Travelling to work in a sweaty tube carriage so hot that the windows of the train were beginning to melt, I muttered a silent prayer.

"Ugh. I hope it's not this hot when we're walking the Coast to Coast...."

It was an utterance perhaps best left unspoken. As we awoke for our second day of walking, rain was hitting the tarmac on the street outside.

"We've only had to dry walkers' clothes three times since Easter" added the B&B owner helpfully as we surveyed the situation.

Squeezing once more into Catherine's tiny, three sizes too small waterproof trousers (I mean, would it kill her to put some weight on?!) we trudged down the road to Ennerdale Water, certain parts of my anatomy regretting every move.

As it happened the rain had stopped as we reached the waters edge and I quickly decided to adopt plan B. I was going to dispose of the trousers, unzip the legs off my walking trousers and do the day in shorts. If they got wet, well frankly they'd dry out. Eventually. But at least I'd be bloomin' comfortable.

* * *

Ennerdale Water has two routes around it. Along the north shore is an easy, day tripper friendly version whilst Wainwright chose the more challenging path on the south.

Initially easy, we soon found ourselves clambering over slippery rocks, "admiring" the sharp drop down to the rocky waters edge below. There's nothing like a nice gentle start to the days walking, is there?

And then there was the rain. On and off showers did indeed get my shorts rather damp although thankfully the plan was working and half an hour after the rain stopped my shorts were almost always dry. Just in time for it to start again normally....

It was a difficult route. Every time you thought it was getting easier, some more wet rocks to scramble up and over suddenly appeared. The end of the lake couldn't really come soon enough, and we got there as the rain finally stopped meaning we could rest there awhile whilst watching the waves lap gently on the shore edge. The view seemed to make all the effort suddenly worthwhile.

For all our toils in the damp weather, it felt a wrench to leave Ennerdale Water as we crossed some fields to join the road running on the edge of Ennerdale Forest which ran parallel to the River Liza, without actually being close enough to provide a view of it.

Passing by YHA Ennerdale, the first of four youth hostels we'd see on the day, we headed on along the winding road which seemed to delight in going up and down and being enclosed by trees. Every now and then there'd be a gap and we'd be able to glimpse out and see the mighty fell of Pillar over on the other side of the dale, but most of the time it was just us and the leaves.

Still the rain had gone and a little sun had even come out - so much that we parked ourselves on a convenient log and ate our packed lunch whilst putting the world to rights. Well, okay, we discussed how much better we'd be able to run the Shepherd's Arms Hotel compared to the current management. First step would be to get the locals on board - after all, how can a rural pub/hotel really make money when there are no tourists around.

The world sorted - and our stomachs filled - we headed towards the end of Ennerdale and perhaps the finest location of the whole day. A location that also managed to house youth hostel number two: the isolated little hut that is Black Sail.

Wainwright describes Black Sail as "the loneliest and most romantic of youth hostels" and it's not hard to see why.

Completely isolated with no public road access,

it has just three dorms and sits looking tiny and insignificant whilst surrounded by the mighty fells of Great Gable, Green Gable, Pillar and Haystacks.

Whilst the beauty of the setting could not be beat, I was more concerned with popping to the loo and I scouted the building to see if there was one.

But the place seemed locked up tight lest non YHA members managed to infiltrate the facilities, and instead we rested on a bench outside as an army of local chaffinches hopped over in the vain hope of picking up something to eat from us. Given I was eating an apple they didn't have much choice, although days later we found out that the hostel was actually unlocked but had a very stiff door, and inside there were tea and homemade cakes for sale which, no doubt, the chaffinches would have enjoyed!

It didn't matter too much as the birds were better fed by some other arrivals who sat down to eat their belated lunch. The two walkers who had joined us were the same two we'd met the day before and who had pointed out the bagpipes. A mother and daughter, at the time I'd assumed the younger one was in her teenage years but in the pub later that night I'd realised she was in her mid 20s with the year difference seemingly accounted for by the bandana she wore whilst walking.

Noting the miraculous age reducing effects of such headgear I resolved to wear my own as often as possible in the hope of being mistaken for a 20 year old once more. Even if was a 20 year old with a slightly podgy belly....

Rested and relaxed it was time to tackle the next challenge - to climb the steep ascent alongside Loft Beck.

It got off to a good start with our guidebook directing us to ford an insanely busy stream. Quite why our otherwise excellent guidebook decided that was a good idea, who knows. Wainwright's original took a higher path and as we struggled across we could see a steady stream of people taking the far easier "proper" route.

Just as we'd finally made it to the right place, having had to leap over the wide stream, the heavens opened and the rain began once more. A good path had, at least, been made with steps cut into the stone, however once more they were made fun by the wet weather.

Then, almost as soon as it had started, it stopped just as we got near the top. Clouds began to part and a view... oh what a view... Amazing views of all around. Of Ennerdale. Of the mighty fell of Haystacks. Of Scotland and the Isle of Man in the distance. And of the divine looking Buttermere valley in the distance. It was as if the rain had had a tantrum on us, then felt rather embarrassed so resolved to make it up to us...

"Well you've been through all that pain.... I'm sorry.... Here, have a moment to rest.... And enjoy...."

It was a beautiful spot. Almost everyone who made it up ended up just staring almost in disbelief - that there really couldn't, shouldn't, be such beauty. As we walked on, I regularly had to turn round and admire it some more, until we finally came to the point of no return, where we'd have to turn away and leave it for ever and head to Honister, walking down on the old dismantled tramway that used to send slate down from the hills.

The tramway was a strange sight. Raised on an embankment it initially remained resolutely flat whilst the land around it gradually sloped down. It looked like it was about to abruptly end in several places, almost like it just stopped. Eventually it headed downhill, heading steeply down to the slate works near hostel number 3: YHA Honister.

Our guide book perhaps hadn't prepared us for Honister Slate Mine. It informed us "great joy awaits you here" and that if the place wasn't busy we'd see the sign inviting us to take tea for a voluntary donation. It put in mind of a small operation - a tiny hut with someone handling the slate and occasionally chatting to interested tourists.

Instead we found a full on "slate experience" with a full car park, slate experiences, an invite to fill your car boot with slate for £20 and a petition calling for support for a new zip wire!

It all seemed so strange; so wrong. So odd that we felt compelled to endure the tourist trappings of a heart shaped chocolate chip shortbread with our cup of tea from the bustling café.

Resisting the lure of a "I walked the Coast to Coast" slate coaster, a slate picnic table and the chance to put a load of slate in our rucksacks, we set off once more down towards the valley floor; Honister only being a mere staging post on the long descent down hill.

The path meandered gently down hill; far more gently than the main road which passed nearby. Compared with the business of the paths from Black Sail, it was quiet now and we saw few people bar a couple of cyclists heading upwards.

Our route eventually went down hill with a vengeance on a descent that boarded on the near vertical in parts to take us near the village of Seatoller. From there we were on the home straight and a wooded path to hostel 4 and our destination - the beautiful Borrowdale YHA.

There was just one last obstacle - an extremely narrow section of path along the side of the busy River Derwent. One section was so narrow that a chain was provided to hang on to and after safely negotiating it and setting foot on the fractionally wider path on the other side, I mused on how many people have traversed the whole day safely only to believe this to be a trivial section before falling and slipping.

No sooner had I thought that and I slipped on the rocks, falling heavily on my left side, my rucksack trying to drag me towards the river whilst I clung on to the stones for dear life.

Despite the hard landing, thankfully nothing serious happened bar my knee getting a trifle muddy and we made it safely along the remaining hundred metres to the busy hostel where the warden promptly spent several hours going through the many food options available to us during our stay. What would we like for the evening meal? Three course or just one? Porridge for breakfast? Vegetarian sausage? Beans or tomatoes? Packed lunch? Large or small?

Each meal seemed to have its own checklist of options to consider and it was a blessed relief to finally have filled them all in so we could shower and change before actually eating. Still the warden was a very friendly and nice chap and gave us the hire of two towels for free, so one mustn't really grumble.

Hostels have changed a lot since the old days. We'd recently watched a documentary about hostelling of old, full of spotty oiks sarcastically singing "We love you warden, we do" as he tried to impose lights out.

I don't know if hostels did meals then but if they did they no doubt involved a big vat of stew sold at thruppence a bowl. But only if you did your chores and had cleaned the toilets before hand.

Whilst contemplating that thought, we munched on marinated olives, chomped on homemade bread and enjoyed a freshly cooked vegetable curry and Cumberland sausage respectively.

And as we retired to the lounge and supped our bottles of locally brewed, bottle conditioned ales (well Claret didn't seem quite right really), I pondered starting a good old fashioned sing song, handing round copies of the YHA songbook and shouting "Come on everybody!"

Times change and somehow I didn't think the

large group of super-cool looking teenagers doing a jigsaw puzzle would have gone along with the idea. With a heavy sigh I did the next best thing and ordered another bottle of beer and checked on my laundry.

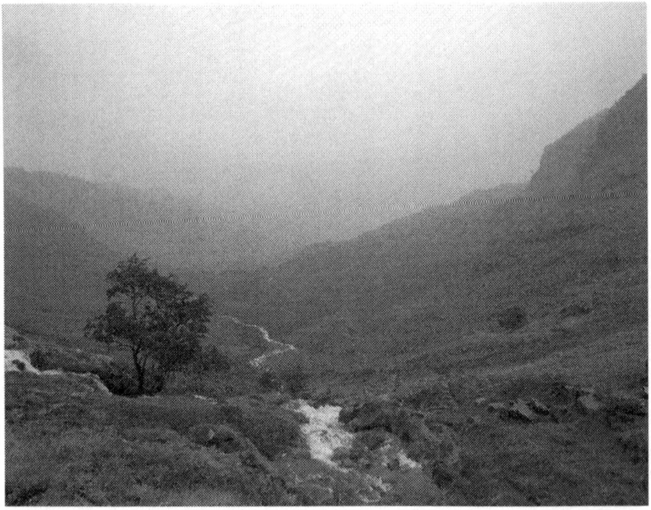

Day 3 - Borrowdale to Patterdale

"I think the YHA should do a butler service. Someone who will sort out all your drying and stuff for you. Yes okay, I know it's not in the true spirit of hostelling, but I'd use it!"

Little is recorded on what clothing Wainwright favoured for walking. Well okay, it might be extremely well recorded but I couldn't be bothered to do any research. It wouldn't have improved anything I'd written, so frankly I'll stick to the assertion above.

In my mind I always have him in tweed although it's far more likely he wore a grey anorak, flat cap and had a flimsy blue plastic pacamac for when it rained.

In contrast the modern walker is spoilt rotten. Outdoor clothing companies offer everything from high tech waterproof jackets which clouds will take just one look at before promptly moving elsewhere... QUICK!, through to antibacterial, sweat-resistant t-shirts that you need to wash less often and also look pretty stylish in the pub in the evening to boot.

But even the amazing feats of the hiking boot with Gore-tex in it is never going to keep you dry if you put your foot down and suddenly find yourself up to your knee in a fast flowing, ice cold stream that's been swollen by heavy rain.

Ah yes, rain. If the wetness of the previous day had felt bad then the next two were to be horrendous. The forecast promised light showers, maybe some drizzle.

The forecast lied.

* * *

It all started reasonably enough as we left Borrowdale Hostel and headed down the road to Stonethwaite. Wainwright's "official" route actually does a little loop round the village of Rosthwaite, but that seemed to be more for accommodation purposes more than anything else so we headed down the road to join the path on the other side of Stonethwaite Bridge. The lovely of the previous afternoon had gone, the fells were covered and the rain was coming down gently. Even so it was a lovely start to the day.

I was in familiar territory having walked up this stretch in the opposite direction the year before whilst doing The Cumbria Way, albeit in much nicer weather.

When we arrived at Smithymire Island we stopped to admire the waterfalls. The rain showers and early time of our arrival (we'd left the hostel at 8:20) meant it was a quiet spot compared to the crowds on my last visit, and I longed to linger but we had a long trek ahead of us.

The exact distance from Rosthwaite to Patterdale seems to be a bone of contention. We'd seen estimates ranging from 14½ miles from our guidebook, through to 19. Wainwright himself lists it as 17¾ but the exact distance varies on which routes you pick - this one simple day contains three points where you can pick between different options and the exact distance depends on whether you make a diversion into the village of Grasmere.

Leaving Smithymire Island (and the Cumbria Way) behind, we started the steady climb up along Greenup Gill.

Recent heavy rains meant the water was crashing down the valley and seeking out new routes to get there - one of which was our footpath.

The further up we got, the more flooded the paths became and things got especially fun as we approached Lining Crag.

A steep, rocky outcrop jutting out by itself, some kindly footpath engineer had made some lovely stone steps cut into the rock. However the very steep path had naturally taken on a new use as a most pleasing waterfall.

The thought of slipping was not a particularly good one given the rocks below, but in many respects it looked far worse than it was and we soon reached the summit and headed towards Greenup Edge.

Up high and deeply in the clouds the weather was getting steadily worse and we were getting a good soaking. My shorts were drenched but even so I was filled with optimism that as soon as the weather cleared, I'd quickly dry off. The forecast had promised heavier rain in the morning before easing to light showers and drizzle in the afternoon. It would be fine.

However the weather was just one of our problems. Our path required us to ford several small streams but in the rain they'd swollen and dramatically expanded.

Shallow stepping stones were suddenly inches below water and several points required huge leaps in order to cross. At Birks Gill even that was impossible and we resorted to huge detours in order to attempt a safe crossing.

After seeing a large party with a dog appearing from the opposite direction, we hoped for some local knowledge to help guide us to the other side. The dog proved it was possible, making a big leap. It almost didn't make it, having to fight the torrent of water to avoid being washed away before eventually climbing onto our side of the bank.

However any hopes of humans giving us a handy tip were quickly dismissed as we heard the cry of "Come on dog! We're not going that way" and the poor hound had to make its way back to join the walkers who strode off in a different direction.

Still if a dog could cross, so could we. Taking a huge run up we just about made it with only a minor soaking.

However the crossing lead us on to Grasmere Common and that resulted in yet more rain and sodden stone paths getting us more and more soaked. When we should have seen the mighty sight of Helm Crag, all we got was grey shadows in the gloom.

By the time we arrived in the valley near Grasmere we were drenched and hungry and we had some shopping to do.

Earlier in the day I'd idly wondered if I could get away without any waterproof trousers however the weather had persuaded me otherwise. After eating our soggy lunch on a soggy bench on the village green (the local burghers having clearly decided that having benches in their attractive stone bus shelters might attract the wrong kind of people) I got my wallet out and marched into the local branch of Cotswold.

In my soaked and muddy state trying anything on would be difficult and I'd prepared myself mentally to pay an insane amount in order to get a decent pair of breathable waterproof trousers, purchased without even trying them on. Which is why I was more than happy to walk up to the shelf and instantly spot the exact same type as I'd accidentally left at home in London and for a reasonable cost. Standing in the doorway I clambered into them and instantly felt a lot better. And warmer.

* * *

Many people break for the day at Grasmere and from experience I'd recommend it - even in good weather the next stretch to Patterdale would see us going more steep climbs over tough terrain.

But with thoughts of the weather forecast telling us that the worst of the weather should be behind us we headed off up alongside Tongue Gill. Catherine had walked the same path the year before and believed it to be good and well made. An easy traverse. Mind you, she'd done it in blazing sunshine...

The low lying cloud had refused to budge and the rain was coming down harder than ever. The paths were horrendous and as we neared the top the streams we had to ford were getting worse and worse.

Water was literally pouring off the hillside by any route it could find. Several new streams had formed and on one outcrop a new waterfall was merrily flowing down over the peat.

The streams we had to ford were mixed with very slippery rocks to scramble up and any pretence my boots gave at keeping out water was well over as I slipped whilst fording and I suddenly found myself up to my knee in the strong flowing water.

My only hope as we reached the top and the Grisedale Hause pass was that going over into a new valley would see an abrupt change in the weather. Our guide book proclaimed it to be a strong possibility and it was right. There was a major change.

The weather got even worse.

Howling winds greeted us as we tried to pass Grisedale Tarn, and the descent down to Grisedale itself was truly horrible. The wind felt like it could pick me up and blow me off the rocky path and crash down onto the beck far below. These were no conditions to be out in, and the weather forecast had left us completely mentally unprepared for it. There was no option but to keep on going. At times I had to resort to crawling on the ground just to try and keep myself from falling. When we finally made it down hill and out of the cloud, all I wanted to do was collapse.

Alas there were still several miles to go - most of which seemed to blur into nothing as we marched as fast as we could for shelter. It was past six and we still had several miles to go. By the time we reached Patterdale I was beyond running on empty.

Exhausted and sodden, we eventually arrived at Patterdale hostel, dripping puddles everywhere we went.

It was 7:30 when we had finally arrived and as such had missed out on the hostel evening meal. The warden told us we'd be able to eat at the nearby pub but they stopped at 8:30 leaving us with just under an hour to sort out our rucksacks, stretch and thrust everything we could into the drying room before rushing out to the White Lion.

Everything was drenched. We'd lined our rucksacks with bin bags and had had our rucksack raincovers on but the sheer amount of rain had worked its way past every barrier. My notebook was a big mess of soggy paper and the notes from the day before, extensively written in fountain pen, had just washed away. Catherine's drawings had faired better but had smudged. A sodden and broken iPod I could have coped with. But this was a heartbreaking sight.

We trudged to the pub and collapsed on a bench. I was mentally and physically exhausted. When our food came I was merely eating as a refuelling exercise - taste just didn't seem to come into my thought process. The beer was good but whether the lamb shank was excellent or awful, well I just can't tell you. I just sat, ate and shook my head at the thought of what we'd just been through, thanking our lucky stars it was all over; that we'd made it safely and were alive.

Thoughts of being winched up to a helicopter on a stretcher had filled my mind half the afternoon. We'd probably never been in any major danger - we were both experienced walkers - however it was by far the worst weather we'd ever walked in and all it would have taken was one small accident.

On the bar was a donation box for the local mountain rescue team. I dug into my pockets and found as many pound coins as I could.

Back at the hostel the weather forecast proclaimed that there would be more heavy rain overnight, clearing in the morning. And sure enough as we headed to bed, the heavens were doing their finest outpouring. Damp and tired we headed for our cold room, collapsed on the bunks and slept... slept... slept very well indeed.

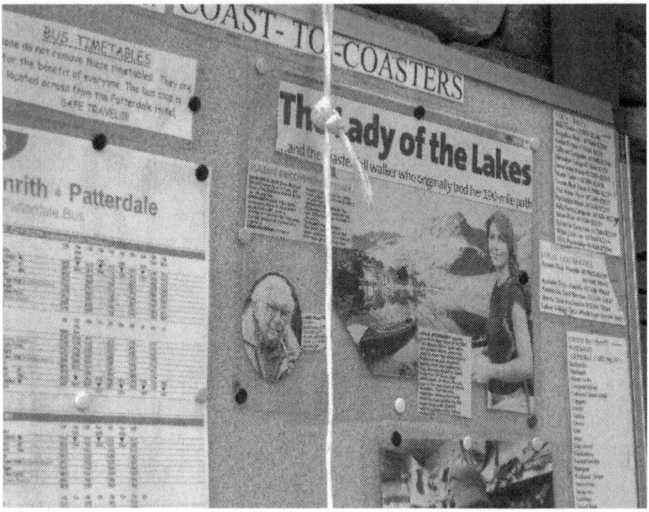
COAST-TO-COASTERS
BUS TIMETABLES
SAFE TRAVELS!
Patterdale
ady of the Lakes

Day 4 - Patterdale to Bampton

"I'm sorry. We're a bit wet..."

I'm not sure I can say I've stayed in a truly awful youth hostel however Patterdale YHA must be getting close. It was cold, damp, grubby and I'm convinced there was more space reserved to corridors than there was to beds.

Built on stilts in some sort of Scandinavian style, the place clearly needed a lot of work to bring it up to some sort of reasonable state. The gents toilets were half flooded, reminding me more of a campsite toilet block. Ironwork and metal girders sat rusting, drops of rain getting through. The paintwork in our room looked like it was covering damp. Oh and when I put my boots on in the glass windowed corridor near the front door, I got a lovely view of a rotting, long dead bird in the outside courtyard.

But in its favour YHA Patterdale has two vaguely redeeming features:

1) it has probably the most comfortable and widest bunk beds in the whole of the YHA network

2) it has a truly amazing drying room

Given how wet our stuff was after the previous day, and how full the room was with residents' clothing, I was astounded that our possessions were all pretty much dry the following morning. Indeed just before breakfast I found a t-shirt and some socks that I'd somehow missed the night before and popped them in. An hour later they were in a pretty good state. It was like some sort of miracle working drying room and given the room didn't feel particularly warm AND had a window open, I've frankly no idea how it did it.

Packing up and hitting the road, we surveyed the drizzle in Patterdale before heading to the village store for some provisions.

Patterdale Village Store is like some sort of Coast to Coast heaven. As well as selling groceries to the locals, it caters well for the walker from its range of freshly made sandwiches through to walking equipment including boot leather waterproofing stuff that I later regretted not buying.

Outside the shop is a C2C notice board featuring a photograph of the new patron saint of the path, Julia Bradbury, who had presented a TV series on the Coast to Coast for BBC Four. Many a pub conversation seemed to turn to Julia's name and how easy she made the whole thing look...

Julia had, naturally, visited the shop as part of the TV programme as it has another important Wainwright connection - it was the first store to agree to sell Wainwright's first pictorial guide. And from those humble beginnings, a legend was born...

Wainwright's decision to route the Coast To Coast may, or may not, have been related to that first purveyor of his wares, although it's far more likely it's because he really loved Patterdale. Either way there's no doubt the Coast to Coast has treated Patterdale well. Unlike the weather which hadn't.

"I've just got back from Sunny London and found a river running through my back garden!" proclaimed a rather over the top posh man in his best Queen's English, who had arrived in the shop. He might as well have added "Wot ho!" for good measure.

* * *

It was a stiff but not too bad a climb out of Patterdale up to Boredale Hause and we walked along a well made path which seemed to have no major ambitions of providing water flow. Despite it being a Monday the climb was full of walkers, most of whom dispersed in different directions at the top of the first ascent and many of whom seemed to be clutching copies of various Wainwright guides.

We'd now entered into the cloud and the light drizzle had turned almost imperceptibly into showers. Having not put on my new, shiny and well fitting waterproof trousers, my legs were soon wet once more and a good stiff wind meant that trying to put them on would have been at best a futile endeavour and at worst, a good slapstick comedy routine for anyone watching. Cloud cover meant that the views were limited and by the time we reached the beauty spot of Angle Tarn, we were seeing very little at all around us. The tarn itself was almost invisible in the gloom until we were almost right on top of it.

The rain was biting, almost whipping our faces and a good walk had quickly turned into trudgery. The higher we got, the worse the rain and wind got.

Passing by the putrid remains of a dead sheep (cause of death presumably drowning) we found an almost miraculous gap in the cloud. All of a sudden we could see for miles around. The wind had gone, the rain disappeared. Down below, Hayeswater glistened. Then, all of a sudden, the views were gone, the rain back, the wind trying to blow us over once more.

Wet and wind weary, we clambered over the soggy rocks of "The Knott" and passed down to the almost Tolkein-esque Straits of Riggindale, before abruptly turning north east towards Rampsgill Head.

For a moment it seemed like the direction change would reward us with better weather however by now we should have known not to get hopes up too high. As we approached the highest point of the "normal" Coast to Coast walk (normal being the version where you didn't take any insane high level alternatives in the Lakes) at Kidsty Pike (780m above sea level), the weather was at its worst.

It was all downhill from here but our boots - now letting in water like there was not only no tomorrow, but no day after either - were sodden; our socks like sponges, just letting it all in.

I was already fed up and miserable, but now I had to contend with a steep descent as well and I was having real trouble. My feet were slipping and sliding around inside the boots and I was having serious trouble regulating my speed. I'd try to come down slowly, then my socks would slip and I'd find myself coming down far too fast, with little to no control over my speed - seriously really not good on the steep, slippery rocks. I had images of trying to come down slowly but somehow finding that my feet were forcing me down at running speed. Oh hang on, that DID happen, and it took an almost Herculaneum effort to do an emergency stop. Oh and one of my walking poles had broken.

Damp, cold and fed up, I slammed my rucksack on the grass and sat on a rock. Struggling in the rain to take my boots off so I could wring out my socks, I lost my rag and ended up shouting my frustration across the valley. The two horrible days of rain and the constant rain on the Pennine Way earlier in the year had taken their toll. It was summer. The country was in a heatwave. There was a hosepipe ban. Yet here was I removing half a pint of water from my boots. We later found out that the Lake District had had a whole months rain in two days. And we'd been out in every minute of the worst of it. If someone had turned up and said "Helicopter to London for Mr Bowden", well I would have gone straight back home and no mistake.

At least the sock de-watering session had helped. My feet were still cold and damp, but I could at least make it down hill without slipping, but as we made it to the valley floor at Bowderthwaite Bridge

I was in extremely bad mood. Wainwright's name was cursed under my breath. He'd written "A Coast To Coast Walk" after experiencing the "horribleness" of the Pennine Way, but after the last day and a half I was seriously wondering what the difference was. This was a nightmare of walking and my mood didn't lift much as we attempted to eat our lunch in a soggy wood just off the trail.

The driving rain - which according to the forecast should have been, at worst, drizzle by now - penetrated even the dry plantation floor. We'd barely rested all morning and even here there was no shelter and little rest for two weary walkers.

* * *

From thereon in the walk was alongside Haweswater Reservoir. Created in the 1930s to supply water to Manchester, it extended a smaller lake and drowned the village of Mardale.

There was a hosepipe ban in force and the reservoir level low, but water was streaming down hill as fast as it possibly could. The winding reservoir-side path was a huge stream; every step making our boots wetter and wetter.

For me, the salvation at the sight of the end of the reservoir was much appreciated. Most people press on another four miles to Shap - a fifteen mile day followed by nineteen the next - however we'd spotted that we could break the two long days up in three more comfortable ones by stopping at Bampton and then Orton before arriving at Kirkby

Stephen. The reservoir end meant our turn off to Bampton and the simple trek up a main road to the pub we were staying in.

My gloom began to lift, raised even more so by the odd sight of an old signpost marked MCWW - Manchester Corporation Water Works - which had somehow lasted all these years even though the MCWW had been absorbed into North West Water in 1973. Something about this long surviving sign amused me. And to cheer me up even more, a sight that would raise the spirits of even the most drenched walker. For there in the middle of the road sat a very relaxed looking red squirrel! We abruptly stopped. It looked at us briefly then scampered into the undergrowth, its work done.

Maybe it was that we were on the home stretch. Maybe it was the squirrel, but even in the non-stop rain, I felt invigorated as we passed through the model village of Burnbanks, originally built to house the workers building the reservoir in the 1930s, and as we arrived at the Crown and Mitre in Bampton, there was a spring in my step - even more so when we found out we'd been given a better room than the one we'd expected.

After the best shower we had on the whole trip, we had the best meal too as we ate some absolutely amazing food. It was so good that we had three courses. Any place that can make me enjoy baked figs had to be credited and my sea bass in prawn and saffron sauce was amazing. I'm not even a fan of Brulee but the Raspberry Brulee they served was divine. And whilst the other two handpulls were off, the Black Sheep was extremely well served.

You get used to "pub food" on long distance walks. It can be good, it can be awful. But it's pub food. And usually served with chips, chips and more chips. Well here in the middle of Cumbria, on the edge of the Lake District, was a pub with the most outstanding bistro style dining, big portions and great prices to boot. It was like manna from heaven. It's so good I wholeheartedly recommend making a HUGE detour just to eat there. Hey, 100 miles should do it!

And hey the place was so good that we went to the expense of having our sodden clothes tumble dried. And that was probably the best £5 we spent on the whole trip.

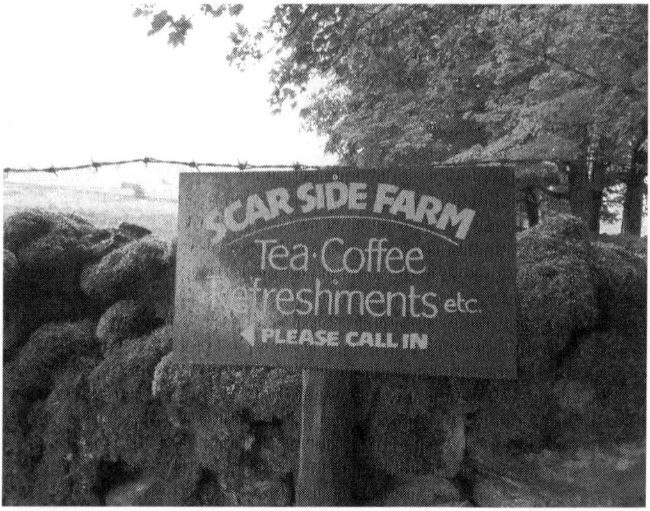
SCAR SIDE FARM
Tea·Coffee
Refreshments etc.
PLEASE CALL IN

Day 5 - Bampton to Orton

"A man with a flat cap. That's made it into a proper pub now!"

There's nothing worse when you're walking than waking up to yet another miserable day of rain. And that's what I woke up to. At 3am.

In contrast by the time we left around 9:30 the rain had stopped and it was looking like a reasonable day as we strolled out of Bampton.

Bampton's not actually on the Coast to Coast - it's about a mile north-east of it and taking a look at the map we worked out we could cut off a corner. If we headed down the road, south-east, we'd meet up and just miss about a mile or so of the "official" route.

Given we'd be mostly missing walking over farmland and Wainwright himself was quite in favour of making your own route (hence why he called it "A Coast to Coast Walk" rather than "The...", although it is a slight contradiction with the incredibly detailed, prescribed routes detailed in his books), we didn't feel too bad about it. And as we strolled down the road ready to meet Wainwright at the village of Rosgill, there was a spring in our steps. It was warm, it was dry and we had a pretty easy day in front of us.

We'd left the difficulties (and bad weather) of the Lake District with its high fells and rocky paths, and now most of our days would be sensible 11-12 mile trips without too much up and down.

Walking over dry and pretty looking farmland we arrived at Shap Abbey, the ruined remains of a medieval abbey with its striking 15th century tower which, given the bad state of the rest of the place, has remained almost intact since old Henry VIII had his tizzy with Rome and went after the monasteries with a vengeance.

Leaving the atmospheric Abbey behind us, we left something else behind us too - the Lake District. At long last we left the National Park, and given how badly the weather had treated us during our visit, frankly I was glad to see the back of the place as we walked on to Shap proper.

For most people Shap is the end of a hard days slog from Patterdale and the beginning of a 20 mile trek to Kirkby Stephen. In contrast when we arrived around half eleven, the place was pretty clear of walkers. We stopped off at a local newsagents, bought sandwiches and had an early lunch sat on a bench on the A6, reasoning we should eat whilst we could and whilst it was dry! Doing so almost inevitably meant the rain would stay clear of us for a few more hours, and we could have had lunch in far nicer surroundings...

Wainwright considered that the Coast to Coast was split into three parts by the M6 motorway at Shap and by crossing the A1 near Richmond. With my public transport agenda I preferred the idea of using the nearby West Coast Mainline as my third-way point, and in celebration a train load of groceries passed us by bound for Tesco, hauled by a train branded as "Stobart Rail". On the motorway shortly afterwards an Eddie Stobart branded lorry proclaimed it was "delivering sustainable distribution" and we both looked at each other and wondered what on earth that meant when linked to lorries thundering up the M6.

Passing into a field on the other side of the motorway we were joined by a procession of horses who were either inspired by us to walk the same way, or just happened to be passing in our direction.

They had a good sized field, shared with some sheep, but seemed keen to cross our path at speed at a time that just happened to coincide with our arrival.

Half expecting a stampede to form, we edged closer and closer to the stile, just before which the horses broke off their pursuit, suddenly content to graze at some grass under a tree. It was no doubt an act they put on for all the walkers.

Leaving behind views of Shap's quarry, cement works and the noise of the M6 we headed on to the moorland of Crosby Ravensworth Fell, although its heather lined ground was never too far from more grassy pastures.

From a superb limestone pavement just off the Roman road of Wicker Street, we were presented with fine views of the North Pennines and worked out a gap on the horizon was High Cup Nick near

Dufton, a mighty and deep U-shaped valley sat gently in the moorland; a fantastic place we'd visited a few years before on the Pennine Way.

The views were so fine, we sat down and enjoyed them before the buzz of our mobiles distracted us. Having been in mobile free areas for several days, suddenly a batch of messages and missed calls came in mainly relating to Catherine's brother and his wife who had also happened to be in the Lakes whilst we were there and had wondered if we'd be able to meet up. Naturally they took our radio silence as a no.

After a nice sit down and some chocolate, we headed on once more passing by a large mound of stones known as Robin Hood's Grave - the second time Sherwood's famous son had supposedly made appearance on our walk, although why he'd be buried up here is frankly anyone's guess, and to most modern eyes the place would just look like what it actually was: a large, oversized cairn.

It had been relatively dull but dry most of the day but now the heavens opened as we met a minor road a few miles from our destination of Orton and we quickly donned waterproofs and headed off the moorland and over the farm fields that would take us there.

A sign invited us to visit Scarside Farm for refreshments and whilst tempting, it was on the alternative route that bypassed the village and our room at the George Hotel was waiting for us. After quickly admiring the limestone tower of the local church and detouring into the village shop to stock up on bin-bags (for lining our rucksacks) we arrived at the pub to see the depressing sight of the doors bolted, the lights out and the doorbell missing.

Blu-tacked to the door was a note telling us to ring a phone number to be let in however once more mobile reception had departed us and just as I was about to dash across the road to the phone box opposite, two walkers appeared out of the blue and nabbed it.

Given payphones across the country are under threat due to lack of use, it seemed incredible to be in an old fashioned pay phone queue. It was a long wait. The phone call went on. And on. And on. So long that one of them wrote "Help me" on the steamed up glass. Yes well, I thought. What about me? It was agonising to be so close to our room and yet to be so far. We were stood on the pub doorstep for nearly twenty five minutes before I managed to get into the box where I promptly discovered the confounded thing wasn't taking coins leading to more faff of trying to enter debit card details on a malfunctioning number pad.

It seemed rather excessive to pay £1.20 just to get inside, but eventually we were shown to our room which was furnished with a four poster bed, a wobbly floor that made you feel drunk every time you walked across it, and radiators that were on full blast even though it was a mild July day. Such heat was glorious given it meant we could finally dry our boots out, and we set about filling the room with laundry and wet leather.

Feeling more refreshed (although wondering

why a room with a four poster bed didn't come with any shampoo) we adjourned to the rather chilly bar for a few hours before making our way back upstairs and letting the floor do what the beer and wine hadn't. We stumbled on to the king sized mattress and sank into a rather warm sleep, safe in the knowledge that, if nothing else, our clothes would be very, very dry the next day...

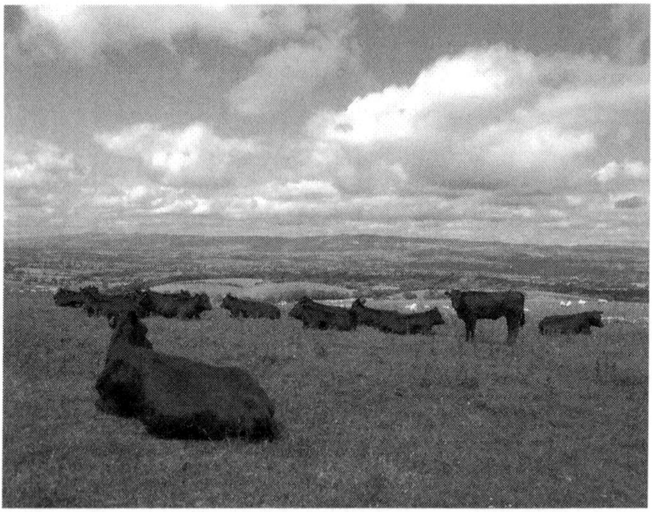

Day 6 - Orton to Kirkby Stephen

"You put your waterproofs on and five minutes later it stops raining! Ridiculous!"

"Did you hear on the local news about those four teenagers at Ennerdale Bridge? They got stuck in the rain - one of them tried to cross a swollen stream and got trapped. Another had to get in and try to get her out. Had to get Mountain Rescue out in the end to rescue them all."

Such cheery news was the conversation with two fellow walkers over breakfast. They were fellow Coast to Coasters, finishing off their trip at Kirkby Stephen later that day. They told us they hadn't decided if they were going to come back and finish it off, although if you ask me, they were pretty much a shoe in.

The rain in the Lakes would be the subject of many a discussion over the next few days with walkers we met, whilst newspaper headlines would loudly decry the fact that despite the heavy rain, North West Water had no intention of lifting the hosepipe ban. It was during one of those conversations that we found out that a whole months rain had fallen in those two wet and soggy days.

And as we left Orton, popping once more into the most excellent village shop (with its amazing cheese selection) there was a slight dampness in the air, although nothing too serious as we clambered once more over stiles and headed over fields to Ravenstonedale Moor.

Whilst there was occasional drizzle, we mostly had a dry morning until we arrived at Stony Head Farm when the heavens opened. Sheltering under some handy trees, we dutifully struggled into waterproofs. But no sooner had we done so and set off and the rain abruptly stopped. Serenity was restored.

Given the effort we'd gone to, forcing on rucksack covers and fighting to get into waterproofs, we felt almost compelled to keep the confounded things on but the sun was trying to come out, and barely a mile across Tarn Moor we were getting far too hot. Stripping off again was the only option.

Back in Wainwright's day this particular section required a hefty trek up north-east, round a hairpin bend before doubling back on an unrewarding tarmac road, but thankfully the modern day walker can take a far more civilised and direct path towards Sunbiggin Tarn instead, where swans and waterfowl rest. Apparently. We never got close enough to see any of them.

Ravenstonedale Moor was hardly wild moorland; just gentle greenery watched over (and munched) by sheep and cows. Bar them and ourselves, there was no one around, at least until a couple of RAF fighters stormed overhead at such a low height that their bullseyes and serial numbers were alarmingly visible!

One of the best picnic spots in the area - a raised hump above an underground reservoir - was taken, however a rocky crag not too far on also rewarded us with fine views of the local neighbourhood including the nearby Howgill Fells, and the Severals Village Settlement; a complex of prehistoric villages of which all that can be seen now is a series of grassy mounds. If you didn't know already it was the site of an ancient habitation, well you'd walk on by and be none the wiser. The site itself has never been the subject of an archaeological dig and its secrets remain untouched and underground.

More noticeable history came not long after in the tell tale cutting of a dismantled railway and as we took a U-shaped tour of the area, the mighty Smardale Gill Viaduct crossed a ravine in the distance.

Some would say such a viaduct was a scar on the landscape but for me the old Victorian arched railway bridges seem to show man's dominance of the landscape in a highly pleasing way, and provide a fitting tribute to the blood, sweat and tears that built them in the first place, to say nothing of the lives that were lost in the process.

If the views of Smardale Gill Viaduct weren't enough to enjoy then the sight at the top of Smardale Fell was even better. A truly wonderful view of the relatively unknown Eden Valley, and the North Pennines behind it.

So much attention is paid to the undeniable beauty of the Lakes that the Eden Valley often gets overlooked. But it shouldn't, and it deserves to be equally as famous. Nestling between two mighty ranges of fells it has amazing scenery all around and is a fine place to walk through. Yet our guide book seemed almost completely oblivious to it, even if we did linger gladly before making the gentle descent in to Kirkby Stephen.

On our approach, down near an alleyway, a mother sat picking wild raspberries with her young daughter.

"Are they allowed to pick them too?" the daughter asked as we popped a few into our mouths, and it was hard not to smile as her mother explained the laws of wild growing fruit before Catherine gently replied "We've only had two!"

She was lying and it was a lie that would hurt the child and challenge their faith in society for evermore. For in reality we'd not had two, but three. The anguish we must have caused would result in sleepless nights for weeks to come.

* * *

Apparently Kirkby Stephen has a "Welcome to Walkers" accreditation for, well, its welcome to walkers and we got a fine welcome from Denise who owns and runs the local hostel.

Sited in an old Methodist chapel in the heart of the high street it was opened in 1981 yet just 26 years later the YHA had tried to close it down.

Thankfully its future was secured by new owners taking it on so it remains a hostel and whilst independent, it remains affiliated to the YHA who continue to provide roughly 50% of its customers.

It was an amazing conversion with the old organ and pulpit remaining, and the balcony area converted into a lounge. Our room - part of the old warden's quarters presumably, given the wooden "Warden" sign on the door - featured a segment of a stained-glass window.

For a weekday night it was pretty busy and like many of hostels the YHA tried to close in 2006, you couldn't help but wonder why they had ever wanted to sell it off. The new owner seemed happy with her lot, proclaiming it was a job for life and she loved meeting people who were on their holidays. Given its near perfect location for cyclists and Coast to Coast walkers, it's hard to imagine her not having a steady stream of customers for years to come.

* * *

Kirkby Stephen was by far the largest place we'd passed through so far on our trip and had the added luxury of an Indian restaurant. After several days of pub food we both longed for something completely different and given how many familiar Coast to Coast faces we saw inside, we were not the only ones. The Mango Tree offered a fine curry too. Often rural curry houses aren't up to much but this was a cracker and no mistake.

Well fed, we retired back to the hostel to consult

maps and discuss options for the next day before falling into yet another long, deep sleep... Why, anyone would think we'd done some exercise or something...

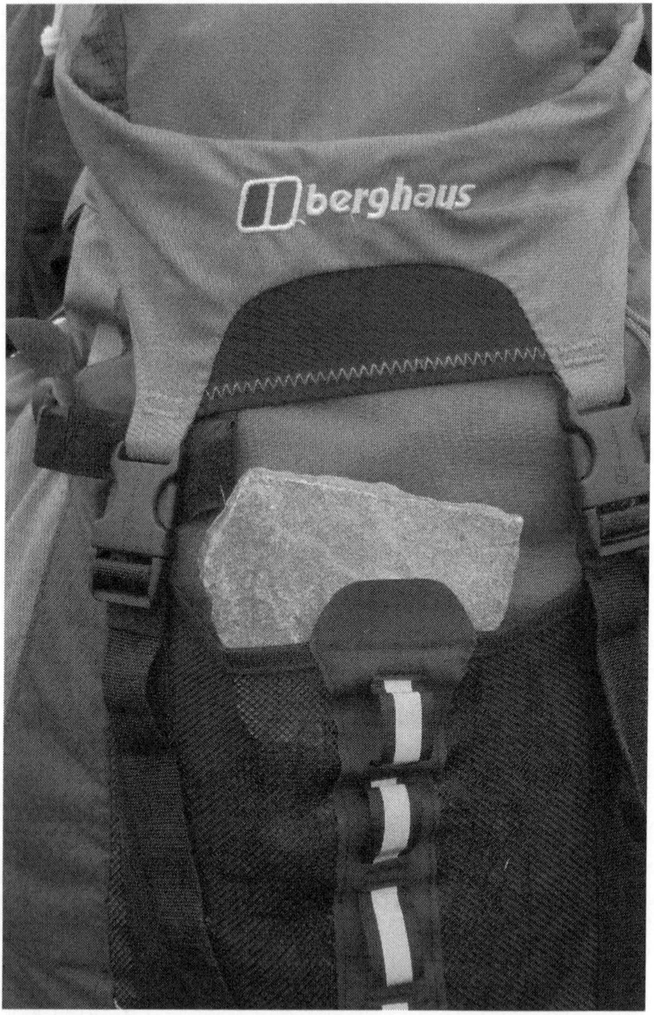
berghaus

Day 7 - Kirkby Stephen to Keld

"This bog is nothing - NOTHING! - compared to the Pennine Way."

Kirkby Stephen is apparently well known for its parrots. A local bird enthusiast keeps them and allows them to fly around town. Apparently they especially like to hang around the chippy. Wandering around the town the previous evening I'd kept my ears open, but every time I leapt around having heard a loud SQUAWK! I saw nothing but sparrows...

And it was certainly not parrots that work me up at 4am with their dawn chorus coming through the hostel window. All the local birds seemed to have camped out just outside making sure I spent the early hours awake and listening to them. Oh and Catherine's snoring too.

At a slightly more reasonable hour of the morning we set off on the relatively easy eleven mile trip to Keld, the first few of which were up a winding tarmac road towards Nine Standards Rigg which gave us fine views back down to the Eden Valley below.

We were part of a merry procession of walkers including an older man out with his dog. The man seemed to spend his time talking non-stop to the small canine, feeding it with historical and local information, almost as if he ran a local history group for pampered pooches. If it could write and talk, no doubt his four legged friend would have done very well in its GCSEs.

Whether said creature cared that the large standing cairns of Nine Standards were rebuilt for the millennium is not recorded, although we sure found the information interesting.

The exact reason why there are nine giant cairns on the hill top is not known, although one theory believed plausible is that they were placed there to make it look like an army was camping there should the old "marauding Scots" try to invade, and the shape of the cairns does suggest tents and sentries.

Other theories - perhaps more mundane - include that they were to mark the boundary of the old Westmoorland county but whatever the reason, their secret is very safe now.

We arrived at the Nine Standards just in time for the cloud to come down and we spent several hours enjoying its all encompassing company, although thankfully rain didn't join it. As we left the cloud had sufficiently covered the Nine Standards enough to just make them look like dark shapes in the gloom as we passed out of Cumbria and into North Yorkshire.

Like many a popular long distance path, heavy usage has taken its toll on parts of the Coast to Coast and nowhere more so than the route down to Swaledale.

Such are the erosion problems on the peaty, boggy moorland, that the Yorkshire Dales National Park requests that Coast to Coast walkers go by different routes depending on the time of year, thus helping the land to recover. Although not compulsory by any means, most Coast to Coasters are naturally happy to comply.

It being July we had the privilege of using Wainwright's original route; a month later and we'd be going somewhere very different.

We were expecting the worst though; horror stories of this section were going round, like the tale of two Americans who had walked in the opposite direction and had had so many problems on the peat bog that they'd just given up at Kirkby Stephen and headed off somewhere else.

However such things are in the eyes - or should that be the feet? - of the beholder and having survived the quagmire that is the Pennine Way in March, it thankfully all seemed rather tame.

Even so it wasn't an easy crossing and life seemed to enjoy making "fun" for me. One of my walking poles broke, the elasticated string on one of my gaiters snapped and I tripped up badly about six times - several of which saw me stuck like a tortoise on its back, unable to right myself without taking my heavy rucksack off.

That aside, the day was relatively straightforward and as we lost height, we lost the cloud too. By the time we passed the 400th Black Hill in the North of England (come on hill namers - show some imagination please!) we were positively on fire dealing with the handful of fords like they were nothing at all.

Indeed we soon found ourselves not that far from Keld, as had many others who had clearly decided that they were too early so took the opportunity to take cream tea at a nearby farm. Catherine's "emergency bog crossing stone" - a large flat piece of rock dutifully carried from near Nine Standards - remained completely unused and eventually found a new home on the hillside.

* * *

Oven Mouth was the next landmark; an amazing ravine looking down on Whitsundale Beck, with farm fields filled with old barns, the upper of which would have held the hay and the lower the animals.

Joining the road to Keld, we slowly came down to Swaledale, stopping only to admire the divine Wain Wath Force Falls. Although Wainwright listed this route as the main walk, he actually recommended a slightly higher route however this would mean missing the falls and frankly they were too good to miss.

Situated just off the road, most walkers passed them by however it was a little ocean of calm as the water sprayed over and fell a distance that can have been no more than a metre in height. The greenery and the setting made up for it and it was a delight to sit there and soak it all in.

We were now barely half a mile from our destination of Keld Lodge.

Back in 2006 it hadn't just been Kirkby Stephen hostel that the YHA tried to close. Indeed a huge number fell under their axe and although many have survived as YHA affiliated independents, Keld was not to be one of them.

Given Keld is on the crossing of the Coast to Coast and the Pennine Way, and given the tiny village has very limited accommodation, it's frankly beyond belief that the YHA couldn't have made Keld Hostel pay its way.

Instead the place was bought at auction and turned into a most pleasant hotel with restaurant and the first pub licence in the village for nearly 50 years after the original pub was bought by a Temperance campaigning Methodist preacher who turned it into a private house.

Whilst a private bunkhouse has opened since, it had been full when we tried to book and there are only about three B&B rooms in the whole village so it was at the former hostel we were booked into, and whilst the most expensive accommodation (marginally) of our trip, it was a lovely stay. The whole place had been superbly refurbished, and retained an excellent drying room.

Its three handpulled ales and excellent food went down so well that we had three courses once more and several pints whilst watching some young 20 somethings from Surrey play a card game called San Juan and argue about Victory Points. You know it's a good game when you have Victory Points.

Keld was also our half way point both in miles and days. We'd gone seven days and had seven more to go. I'd like to say we were getting leaner and meaner, but well that's fried breakfasts and beers for you. Still, that San Juan game didn't half look good.

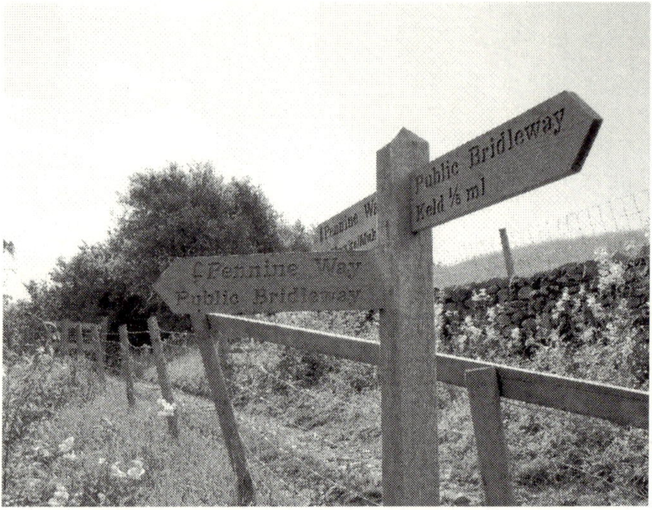
Public Bridleway
Keld 1/5 ml
Pennine Way
Public Bridleway

Day 8 - Keld to Reeth

"Let's see what the old Wainster has to say about that one then..."

It might not look much but Keld is a crossing point for two great journeys. Travelling west to east is the Coast to Coast, and going south to north is the granddaddy of UK long distance paths; The Pennine Way. The two cross at the picturesque Kisdon Force - a series of gorgeous falls just outside the village which we'd last seen some years before whilst doing a long trek up to the Tan Hill Inn on the Pennine Way. It feels like there should be some monument to them both here, but the Coast to Coast isn't even signposted. But then perhaps the waterfalls are enough to celebrate them both.

For both walks Keld is an obvious stopping over point, yet almost everyone staying in this tiny village that night seemed to be doing Wainwright's walk. Where were the Pennine Way walkers I wondered? Perhaps most had pushed on the extra four miles to bunk down at the wonderful Tan Hill Inn where there's always a fire lit, and where ducks and sheep have a habit of popping in for a pint. Or maybe some are down the road at the tiny village of Thwaite. Either way they weren't here.

It wasn't until a few months later whilst doing

the last two days on that route that we found out that actually there just aren't that many Pennine Way walkers out at any one time; even on an August bank holiday weekend we saw just four people walking it. Why, who knows? Maybe everyone was put off by constant talk of dismal weather, of difficulty and of bog. Maybe it was even Wainwright's moaning and whinging about the thing. But at the time all we could do was dutifully wonder at the absence of any Pennine Way walkers, note it down and head off on a fine day towards the capital of upper Swaledale: Reeth.

* * *

Wainwright gives two routes from Keld. There's a low level route which provides a lovely and gentle amble along the mighty River Swale, and there's a high level version which takes in something quite different - the ruins of old lead mines; the legacy of an industrial past.

For whilst now the hills around Swaledale may look peaceful and tranquil, the area was once teeming with activity and Swaledale's lead was used to roof a variety of important buildings including the Tower of London.

The lead industry reached its peak in the area in the mid 18th century as workers hacked out the ore and smelt mills choked the sky with black smoke. It only ended when the industrial revolution saw alternative and more efficient lead extraction techniques developed and eventually the mines closed, the miners left for other parts and the whole area fell quiet bar the grazing of the sheep and, now at least, a steady stream of walkers.

Although he offered and praised the river route, Wainwright recommended the industrial one and after pulling open the curtains that morning and finding the glorious sight of bright blue skies and a very healthy dosage of sunshine, it was this we decided to take and headed off up the hill.

Pausing near the falls to take in a fine view back to Keld and down Kidson Gorge we stopped to chat to a man in his late 60s who was admiring the view. He'd finished the Coast to Coast a few weeks before, camping all the way, and was now back walking selected highlights with his wife.

The weight of my fully laden pack was bad enough sometimes, and the thought of adding in a tent, sleeping bag, food and cooking equipment filled me with dread! That said, when others who were having their bags transported said the same thing to me I'd always point out that by the third day of the walk you barely notice it. And hey if a man in his 60s could do it... Well there's a lesson there.

Slightly further, Crackpot Hall gave the first opportunity to poke around ruins of an industrial past although it wasn't initially built with mining in mind. Built in the 17th Century for the red deer keeper of Lord Wharton, it was later owned by farmers and gamekeepers before passing to officials of the burgeoning mining enterprises. It was mining that lead to its demise; subsidence lead to it finally being abandoned in the 1950s, although signs of its previous life (such as a rusting tin bath) remained on the hill side.

From there the path arched round to the Swinner Gill Lead Mines accessed via a tricky, rocky and narrow path with a sharp drop to the valley floor just near by. Passing by the ruins of the lead mine buildings the path got progressively narrower, muddier and rockier, throwing in some interesting clambering on the rocks, although nowhere near the evil treks the Lakes provided a few days before! And a bad ford before joining an extremely well made and wide path was celebrated by my boot going down nicely into a huge pile of mud.

Walking along the moor tops, we pulled off the nice road and headed down a rather hidden path to the ruins of the third mine: Blackethwaite Mine. Sat in a picturesque valley near Gunnerside Beck, the ruins of an old peat store had an almost cloister like look and feel, giving the impression that the walker had stumbled across the ruins of some long gone church, cathedral or monastery.

It was an idyllic and peaceful spot and the ideal one to heave the rucksacks to the floor and celebrate the passing of luncheon before appreciating that what goes down really must come up, with the very steep climb up to Melbecks Moor and yet another substantial track over the top on a rather bleak and lifeless top that showed the scars of centuries of exploitation. That said there's still activity up there and we passed a JCB and two land rovers before moving to perhaps the mightiest ruins of the day at The Old Gang Smelting Mills

A preserved historical monument with its chimney standing tall and proud, Old Gang offered rusting machinery and rubble strewn buildings. Old Gang managed to hold out until the 1880s and is surrounded by other remnants of its past in the form of numerous spoil heaps.

Further down at Surrender Bridge came our final remnant of the past; the former buildings of the Surrender Mining Company, after which the route reverted mostly to grazed heather moorland, via a ravine with a name that could make Noel Edmonds smirk - Cringley Bottom. Our guide book made it sound like it would subject us to a terror and torment unknown to man outside the Lake District, but in reality it was all rather easy to get down and back up again. We also found a lost walking pole - extracted from just by the beck at the bottom.

* * *

From there it was just us and the sheep as we strolled through farmland and farmyards to the outskirts of Reeth. A lovely village sat around a large green, it was filled with tourists visiting its craft shops and tea shops although by the early evening it quietened down and felt all the better for it. After depositing our extra pole in the tourist information centre we turned up at our lodgings at the Old Temperance which must be the world's only combined B&B and Christian Bookshop.

We'd passed several old temperance hotels on our route, all dating back to a period of our history often forgotten now when social campaigners saw ridding the working classes of alcohol as a way of improving society. The movement grew so strong that it looked at one point that the country would follow the United States of America down the road of prohibition.

The actions of the government during World War I were a prime example - pub opening hours were forcibly slashed, beer severely weakened in strength and nearly rationed in order to stop the workers from not doing their best in the factories. In Cumbria such was the fear of alcohol-related disruption to the munitions factories that all the region's pubs and breweries were nationalised; a grand experiment that wasn't ended until 1973.

In contrast it was World War II that finally buried the temperance movement. Always a bit of a drinker himself, Churchill declared that beer wouldn't be rationed and that pubs would remain open. Indeed pubs were compelled to open their normal hours, hence bombed pubs in London would open the next day with little more than a few barrels on their doorstep if needs be. Churchill recognised the motivational benefits of people being able to go to the pub and relax. In the cities after a night of heavy bombing, one of the first sights people would see as they picked through the rubble was the beer dray delivering to the pubs of the area - even if they didn't need to. It was a sight that showed to the population that life was carrying on as normal.

Pubs became the great social leveller in a way not seen for years. Men and women, working and middle class all mixed in the pub and the temperance movement never recovered. Only one temperance bar remains, in Rawtenstall, Lancashire whilst in Cumbria the National Trust own a temperance hotel. Most had found new uses as homes, as farms or even as B&B-cum-Christian bookshops.

And after a lovely shower and a much deserved cup of tea, we took the temperance message to heart and popped to the pub for a pint. Or two. Well maybe three...

CLOSED
CAMPING
CARAVAN ALSO AVAILABLE
Showers and drying facilities
Evening Meals Menus
Full farmhouse
Elaine's Farmhouse Kitchen
At Farmhouse
Homemade produce
Prize winning
Apple Pie
and Fudge Cake
Savouries
Cream Teas
Hot & Cold
Drinks

Day 9 - Reeth to Brompton-on-Swale via Richmond

"Aye, we get quite a few walkers in here in various states of distress."

Unless you do them camping, one of the problems with doing long distance walks in Britain is food.

The cause is also one of the benefits of walking in Britain - the fact that you can pretty much guarantee you'll be able to pop to the pub in the evening. However that leaves you with the vagaries of "pub grub" night after night after night.

Each region has its own quirks. In the South East of England you may get a pretty varied menu often with rather strange names and lots of "jus" whilst in Scotland everything seems to be heavily deep fried and come with chips. If the majority of the menu isn't burgers and steaks then you're not sure you're in the right place. And then there's the North of England where almost every pub seems to be given a standard menu template to work with, and follows it rigidly.

Without fail the starters will include soup (home-made if you're lucky), that 70s staple prawn cocktail and, for some reason, garlic mushrooms. Meanwhile the main courses will always have an option of some sort of steak pie, fish and chips, steak (sirloin, never rump) and lasagne, preferably served completely swamped in bechamel sauce. They'll probably all come with chips (new potatoes as an option if you're lucky) even if the dish involves a heavy dose of pasta or rice.

And without fail there will be one rather curious omission. An item almost ubiquitous in general cuisine that its absence is almost shocking. For, some reason, the humble beef burger will almost without fail be completely absent without leave. A few weeks after our trip I read an article by beer writer Pete Brown who proclaimed that most pub menus had barely changed since he'd started visiting pubs in the 1980s. Looking at many of the menus on the Coast to Coast, it felt more like the 1970s...

Breakfasts in B&Bs weren't much better. You start the trip going "Fantastic! A full English! Brilliant!" but give it eight of the confounded things in a row and you're suddenly feel your arteries beginning to harden and you begin to wish the place you're staying in would at least offer something different - kippers, a continental style breakfast, salmon and eggs... hey, frankly even just a poached egg instead of fried. Anything but another plate of deeply fried pork products where the only differences are whether you'll get black pudding or beans.

Oh and then there's packed lunches... When we'd walked in France a few years earlier packed lunches were a delight. Every morning we'd be given these wonderful bags containing all manner of stuff. Little tubs of salad, a big hunk of cheese, a little ham, a pile of fruit and a nice little yoghurty thing. And without fail there would be a great big whacking piece of delicious French baguette. It was a culinary triumph of walking food.

Pity the poor French walkers who arrive in Britain and get a round of sandwiches made on dodgy bread with a choice of cheese, ham or egg mayo, coupled with a packet of crisps (never a flavour you like) and a piece of fruit, usually a banana (wich I hate.) If you're lucky - and I mean really lucky - you might get a cereal bar or some chocolate.

And so the long distance walker in the UK enjoys, nay revels, in variations when they come along. At Bampton we lapped up the delicious bistro style food of the Crown and Mitre. In Kirkby Stephen we happily scoffed down a great curry, and the morning after rushed out to the Co-op opposite the hostel for a breakfast of bread and cheese. And at Keld Lodge we had the option of adding in a portion of home made cake into our lunch.

Reeth too had offered a culinary change at the Buck Inn with the inclusion of braised rabbit on the menu which the landlord proudly proclaimed had been running round the hills just a few days before. Meanwhile at the Farmers Arms in Brompton-on-Swale - our destination for this days walking - the special was pan fried mackerel with horseradish crushed potatoes and a tomato salsa.

But that meal was a long way ahead of us - about sixteen miles, including a visit to the largest settlement on the whole route - the town of Richmond.

* * *

Reeth wasn't just full of walkers as we left that Sunday morning, as bike after bike after bike passed us by on some sort of motorcross route, and our path took us right through their makeshift caravan park where grown men pootled around on very small bikes, revving their engines with glee.

We were beginning to leave the hills behind and our day's route was mostly through farmland and grassy tracks. We passed by Marrick Priory, an old home of Benedictine nuns until Henry VIII got into his strop with the Pope and shut the place down. Some of the old priory buildings remained in place, more recently supplanted with more modern creations with somehow managed to blend in with the old stonework despite being pebble-dashed.

The building now houses an outdoor activity centre and we passed a few minutes idly watching a small child climb up a tall tree then go down a zip wire. A respectful hush kept the kids on the ground in awe as he weaved his way to the top before coming zooming down again. All of a sudden there was a mad clamber to be the next one up.

Our route was slightly easier even with a steep ascent up the "Nun's Stairs": stone slabs placed in a wood to allow the nuns to get up to the hamlet of Marrick above their priory. Wainwright totalled the steps as 375 and who were we to argue. Marrick itself was quiet and deserted. Passing by a converted chapel and then a converted church, it was hard not to ponder on the former religious zeal of the place.

The only zeal we saw was a bird desperately trying to get out of a phone box that it was stuck in. Flapping its wings and banging on to the glass, I naturally attempted a rescue by opening the door only for the bird to suddenly discover the route it got in by dropping to the floor and strolling out under the gap, thus making me feel rather useless to the endeavour.

Leaving the hamlet a sign proclaimed we could get refreshments at a nearby farm. This happens quite a bit on the Coast to Coast where farmers have set up facilities to rake a little extra money in from the passing walkers, many of whom are more than happy to stop off for a refreshing cup of tea and a slab of home made cake. We met two walkers who spent their day planning where to eat cake next - be it at a pub, a cafe or a farm. It was their way of breaking up the walking.

Normally we didn't stop, usually making use of ample provisions carried on our backs, but we'd had heard good things about "Elaine's Country Kitchen" and indeed the sign near the farm proclaimed it sold an award winning apple pie. It was also supplanted by a slightly smaller sign proclaiming the place was closed. A double whammy followed as we entered the village of Marske a few miles one where we found out that the local tea rooms were bizarrely closed for refurbishment at the height of the walking season.

I walked through Marske looking out for the "Temperance Farm". It was significant due to formerly being yet another Temperance Hotel that was so popular that it was soon out of business.

The hotel itself was formerly the Dormouse, the village pub, until some point a few years before World War I when one rowdy night in early November a group of carters got drunk and made a huge bonfire of all the wood and wooden objects they could find in the village. The local landowners got the pub licence revoked and the village's new alcohol free future was created. Like Keld, the village had been dry ever since.

* * *

After all these days of walking, going up hill seemed to have got no easier, even the relatively gentle climb up to Applegarth Scar which at least rewarded us for a fine view of the valley for our efforts.

After a slightly dull looking morning the sun had come out and it was baking hot and, after walking along more fields, it was with delight that we popped into a nice and cool wood, and with sadness when we popped out again. Still, leaving the forest meant we got a fine view overlooking the town of Richmond, by far the largest settlement on the Coast to Coast, with its dramatically positioned castle sitting above the banks of the River Swale.

Wainwright kept the Coast to Coast away from

big towns, but with Richmond he couldn't resist the lure of its history. However on a busy Saturday afternoon with the town market in full swing, it all came as a bit of a shock to the system, with the place just being full of people. Most of them seemed to be shovelling their faces with chips as if they'd just come out of some sort of Northern England cliché.

With our huge rucksacks on our backs we were like ducks out of water and when a man asked out of the blue if we were doing the Coast to Coast, my first presumption was that he thought we'd lost the path and couldn't work out where to go. Instead it turned out he was a fellow walker having a rest day in the town and clearly the busyness was as much as a shock to his system as to ours, even if he had had 24 hours to acclimatise.

It's so easy to get out of the real world whilst walking. Having spent the last week and a bit walking through quiet fields and small villages, we'd got used to mainly seeing fellow walkers and few other people. And here we were suddenly thrust back in to civilisation and finding ourselves wanting to get out of it *very* quickly even if it did mean skipping Richmond's many fine tourist attractions.

* * *

Like our fellow walker, most people stop at Richmond to take in the history, see the sights and eat somewhere other than a pub. However that usually results in a 23 mile trek to Ingleby Cross the next day and even though it's on flat land, it wasn't something we were keen on doing. So when we found out we could stay at a pub five miles along at Brompton-on-Swale, we jumped at the chance and booked the room as fast as we could. (We later found out there's a very good bus service between Brompton and Richmond meaning you could stay in a big town *and* reduce the 23 miles if you wanted to.)

First we had to get there, but escaping Richmond seemed to take an age as the route took us on a winding tour of the river banks around the town. Eventually we left the bustling parks and paths which teemed with both people and rabbits. Oh the rabbits! The landlord at the Buck Inn at Reeth could have had a field day filling his larder for a year at least from the fields near Richmond. It was like some rabbit paradise and added to the diversity of the walk which also included going through fields of crops in; the first fields sans sheep or cows that we'd seen on the walk.

However for our weary feet the sight of the A1 was more welcoming as it meant we'd nearly reached our accommodation for the evening, and had now traversed about two thirds of the Coast to Coast.

Being so close to the busy A1 made me worried that the Farmers Arms wouldn't be a great stop - that it would be some bustling motel type place and that the food would be of the kind best described as "ping and dine" - microwaved plastic rubbish. I had worries that it would be the worst stop of the whole trip and it was with relief to find that the food was home made, absolutely excellent and very well done.

It was also a change to be away from other walkers for the night. On the Coast to Coast you end up in some sort of loose collective of people who happen to be doing the route in the same number of days as you. You can spend your day trying to work out which of the people you'd see in your B&B that night, and where there were multiple pubs, who would choose the same as you.

The Farmers Arms seemed completely devoid of walkers - most no doubt staying in Richmond instead - and we saw just two women who we'd passed a few times and seemed to be walking whilst their husbands (who met them in the evenings) did goodness knows what during the day.

The pub may have been heaving and in full swing on this Saturday night, however it another early night that was calling for us. Sunday would see us finish off the remaining 18 miles of the Vale of Mowbray; mostly a "link path" in Wainwright's grand vision, taking us gently between the Dales and the North York Moors. But whilst it might be a long link, the walking would be flat and relatively easy. Hopefully...

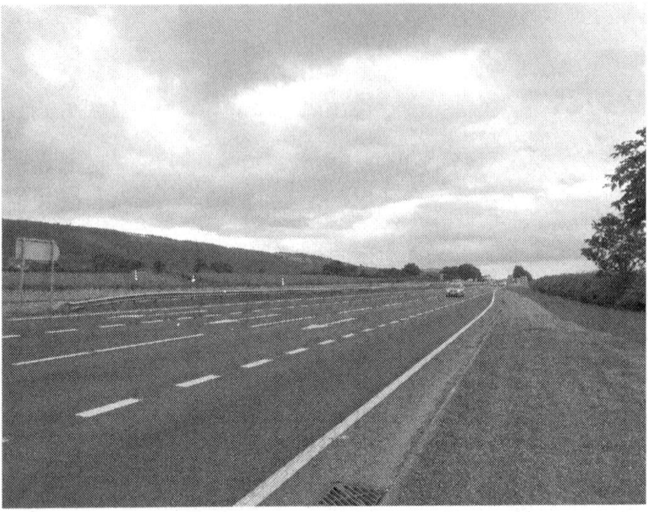

Day 10 - Brompton-on-Swale to Ingleby Cross

"The weather is going to be insignificant tomorrow. No significant rain. No significant sun. No significant cloud. Just insignificant."

At Kirkby Stephen hostel Catherine had spotted a rather elderly guide book for the Pennine Way.

It was, by all accounts, one of the first books written about the granddaddy of long distance paths and at the back it included tips and information for planning your trip, with a sizeable section given over to food, especially packed lunches.

"Packed lunches", it proclaimed, "should include all six of the food groups" and amongst the things walkers were extolled to take were plenty of protein (hard boiled eggs, pork pies, etc.), 3oz of dried fruit and nuts for energy, and of course 2oz of biscuits which, the book felt important enough to point out in case your maths was completely up the spout, meant you should take 4oz for two people *and* that a 8oz pack would last two people two days! Funnily enough it neglected to point out that a large pork pie could last two people two days, nor that if there was two of you, you really should take two boiled eggs...

Every night you should, it went on, have not one, not two but three courses in your meal and you should always start the day with a hearty breakfast.

The commitment to a hearty breakfast was very much in my mind as I sat staring at the gargantuan breakfast placed in front of me at the Farmers Arms.

We'd had a feeling something might be in the offing when the lady serving us proudly proclaimed she'd made the coffee "as thick as tar" and that she'd put three tea bags in the tea pot. She told us this before plonking half a pack of butter on the table and bringing us a toast rack that was so full that the chef had slipped an extra two triangles of bread on the side of the plate.

And then breakfast itself arrived. To say the plate heaved a sigh as it was placed in front of me is perhaps an understatement but let us just say that the only thing they'd skimped on was the solitary egg which sat looking lonely on a pile of fried bread. Then there was the three sausages, three rashers of bacon, two slices of black pudding, a ladle full of beans, fried mushrooms and, of course, a whole tomato.

It was an insane amount of food and felt like a heart attack on a plate. I dreaded the thought of finishing it all, which would probably involve a huge siren and party poppers going off before the chef arrived with a celebratory half loaf of toast by way of congratulation.

* * *

Leaving Brompton-on-Swale was like leaving suburbia; a curious feeling for a walk which Wainwright designed to pass mostly through small villages. However the A1 and Europe's largest military base at nearby Catterick had put their mark on the landscape and our morning was spent wandering along grassy fields near main roads.

Most people try to do this stretch as part of a 23 mile day hike from Richmond. The reason people can do 23 miles in one day - albeit with rather sore feet - is because most of this stretch is flat, going through and along fields and down country tracks. It's not hard to get a good speed up.

It didn't really feel like we were walking along such a busy trail. The paths were often overgrown, looking like they'd seen no one down them for months and months. That said it's far superior to what Wainwright encountered when planning the route. So inaccessible were farm paths due to missing stiles, barbed wire, angry farmers and bulls in the field, that Wainwright routed much of this section along roads. Thankfully due to the work of the council and landowners most of the road walking has now been eliminated.

During the morning we saw very few people bar a father and young daughter cycling, who we encountered mainly due to getting slightly lost near Bolton-on-Swale. Still we did see a highland cow that decided standing in the Swale was a good idea to cool off. Its calf seemed less convinced.

Other than that, the paths were along fields of barley and wheat, and through fields of cows, as we headed to the tiny village of Danby Wiske. One farm at Standhowe offered a small diversion with a sign pointing out what the farmers had done to improve the environment for walkers. It included a notebook for comments and one previous East to West walker had heaped praise on the farm, wishing that some farms from Ingleby Cross had taken a more walker friendly attitude.

After reading that comment I felt a little churlish about potentially complaining about a heavy patch of nettles, and even more so when we passed through a nearby farm where the owners had made the walking as difficult as possible. The path was so narrow that you'd have to walk one foot in front of the other in order to get down it and stiles - when they did exist - were frequently broken. Freshly churned mud was everywhere and random and rusting farm equipment had been dumped right in the right of way. But best of all, a bridge had been made by dumping a 12" wide piece of concrete over a beck, which wobbled ominously as we crossed.

* * *

There had been nowhere at Brompton-on-Swale to buy lunch, and nothing en-route, so we'd had to break the golden rule of the Pennine Way guide book and go out for the day without any food bar half a bag of buttermints. However we knew there was a pub at Danby and a walkers cafe based in someone's house.

Well where the latter was we never did find out.

It seemed to be completely non-existent and we soon grew bored of trying to find it and headed to the pub by default, where a small contingent of walkers and cyclists had congregated for sustenance. The pub sign was clearly Coast to Coast based with one side proclaiming it was 130 miles from St Bees, and the other 60 miles to Robin Hood's Bay.

Given the heat - easily getting above 25°C - orange and lemonade seemed to be the tipple of the day in the White Swan, so much so that the woman behind the bar had to keep rushing off to get new bottles. Refreshing ourselves and lining our stomachs with sandwiches and cake, we were soon ready to set off in the sun once more.

The White Swan had clearly been a crossing place for walkers and there were quite a few who appeared to be going from east to west, however in the afternoon we again saw next to no one bar two walkers late in the day who had presumably set off quite a way away in Clay Bank Top that morning.

The rest of the afternoon was more and more farms. More fields of wheat. More of barley. Field walking's fine but after a while it gets a bit tedious and one of the big problems was that there were few places to rest that either weren't in fields or weren't under the gazing eyes of a farm house. In desperation after crossing a railway line, we ended up sitting down on the concrete steps leading up from the train line.

With few places to stop off for refreshment, some local farmers offered snacks for sale from ice boxes. One gave the curious combination of flapjacks and Lucozade Sport (orange) whilst a later farm gave a choice of fruit, cans of drink or some freshly chilled crisps - clearly important to keep them cold given the way they were artfully arranged over the ice packs.

What I really wanted was a homemade chocolate brownie or some other farmhouse treat, but clearly no farm was in sync with my mind and instead I contend with a tractor whose reversing beeps could be heard for miles around ensuring that everyone knew what was going on even if they were nowhere near it.

Eventually we began to draw near to Ingleby where we'd be resting for the night, and passing by a farm we were greeted by a very happy puppy who would no doubt have followed us all the way to our B&B if we hadn't managed to escape its attention by running as fast as we could.

An even bigger challenge came shortly after and what better way to end the day than trying to get over the six lanes of the horrendously busy A19? Our guide book described it as more dangerous than Striding Edge and I'm not arguing. I'd say it's the most dangerous thing most Coast to Coasters will have to face on the whole thing. There's no crossing, no bridge, no signs to warn motorists, no hope of being able to do anything than hope you've judged the traffic speed correctly and RUN. RUN LIKE THE CLAPPERS. Yes. Run. I don't care what the Green Cross Code says - walking over this thing would have been far more dangerous.

Making it across alive we got to our B&B owned by a fellow Coast to Coast walker who plied us with a fantastic cream tea welcome and proceeded to tell us all about the next days walking before we showered and headed out to the nearby pub only to end up talking to an Australian camper who laid into one hiker who had done 34 miles in one day.

"You'd never seen anything at that speed" he scoffed, despite having proclaimed just moments before he was going to do 30 the next day himself.

As he supped his ale, he didn't seem to be particularly enjoying the Coast to Coast, proclaiming it too busy. He was on a six month holiday in Europe and had only decided to do it after pulling out of a walking route in Turkey after an injury, and having gone to Lancashire to walk random paths just in case they hadn't been used for years and someone wanted to remove their right of way status.

"That must have been interesting," Catherine politely commented.

"Nah. It was just so boring," he muttered with a slightly mad glint in his eye.

The pub itself was far from boring. It clearly hadn't had much money spent on it for years and seemed stuck in a glorious time warp without even having fridges behind the bar. The food was insanely cheap, with most options being about a fiver, but had quite frankly amazing steaks.

Despite being a Sunday evening, it was bustling with locals and after our Australian friend had gone off to get some sleep (having delightedly found there was a marquee he could bivvy down in rather than mess around with his tent) the table next to us was soon colonised by an increasingly large and happy group of dominoes players. As they played I did my best to support the rare cask version of John Smiths. Clearly Smiths was popular - the pub had three versions with the cask version being joined by the miserable Smooth version and the diabolical Extra Cold.

Besides there being two excellent guest ales on, I felt the need to support Cask Smiths in some sort of way, hoping that its international corporate megalomaniac owners would take note of my two pints before deciding to get rid of the stuff.

My duty done we retired to the B&B to try and rest our throbbing feet in the provided foot spa which seemed to do little beside vibrate a lot. Whether it did much to help my feet would just have to be seen in the morning...

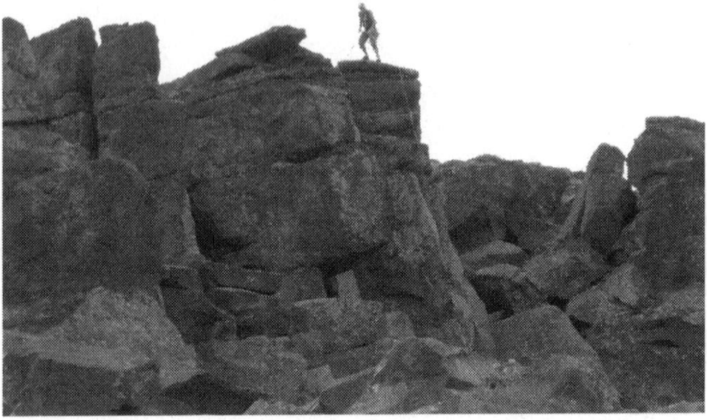

Day 11 - Ingleby Cross to Clay Bank Top

"I'm not sure what a Chicken Parmo is, but Teesside speciality or not, I'm sure you're not missing out on some life changing experience"

I woke up at 2am to major - and I mean MAJOR - league throbbing.

Thankfully it was not my head hurting after four pints of ale. No. It was far worse. My right elbow and left little finger were insanely swollen, itching like mad and feeling very hot. The insects had been after me. Big style.

A friend of mine once proclaimed that if your partner always gets bitten by insects, stick with them as you'll be guaranteed to escape their clutches every time. This might be why Catherine remains with me after all these years. Without fail her skin always remains blemish free whilst every midge, mite and mosquito for miles around will be found beating a path to my door just as fast as they can once they find out that I'm in the area. They probably erect signposts and have marshals to guide other insects on their way to make sure none of them miss out.

Once when we were visiting St Petersburg I woke up one morning with almost every part of my face covered in red blotches - there was barely a piece of skin that was normal coloured. In contrast Catherine had about one bite.

Being the kind of person who makes insects go in to some sort of orgasmic delight, I'd come prepared and had packed the old insect bite relief cream and set about stumbling around the B&B room trying to find it by the light of my watch which emits a surprisingly strong and eerie blue glow when it wants to. Although it does only illuminate a 10mm radius around you.

Banging my feet on rucksacks and tripping over piles of clothes, I finally found the cream and quickly covered myself in as much of the stuff as I could spare and tried to get some sleep. It was going to be a big day in the morning, and not just because I had ordered kippers for breakfast.

Actually I lie. It was because I was going to have kippers for breakfast.

* * *

The sun was shining bright in the morning and as Catherine enjoyed poached eggs and I filled myself with a substantial dose of Omega 3 rich fish protein, the B&B's cat joined in the party by depositing a dead mouse outside the conservatory window whilst two kittens ran amok inside.

Our fellow breakfasters were the mother and daughter we'd been seeing on and off throughout the trip, and who were celebrating the chance to not eat fried pork products by having huge bowls of porridge with fruit and honey, along with homemade bread and preserves. I wondered if the B&B landlady was in her element in this trade, spending her days making jams, scones and cakes with which to line the stomachs of weary walkers.

She knew her stuff too; having walked the whole route herself and being a regular on the sections near Ingleby, she spent much of breakfast telling us not to get confused in the forest above the village. We promptly forgot her wise and sage advice and duly got confused in the forest above the village.

Our saviours were two other Coast to Coasters who proclaimed they'd walked 23 miles from Richmond to Osmotherly the day before and were doing another 15 today. We didn't like to correct them; they'd actually done 28 the day before, and would do 18 today, but they seemed happy enough. Well he seemed happy enough - his partner spend most of the conversation standing a few meters away fiddling with her iPod.

I'd heard about walkers who listened to music as they walked but had never seen one. It's not something I'd seen the point in - why distract yourself from the music of the countryside by playing the music of Beyonce? Although maybe isolating yourself, not letting yourself get distracted by your surroundings, is the only way you can manage 30 miles in one day...

* * *

The first task for the day was to climb the steep but

steady logging road through the woods overlooking Ingleby - which, incidentally, means "village of the English" dating back to when most of the area was filled with Vikings - and on the way we joined the Cleveland Way which we'd follow for the next day and a half.

With the brief excitement of a mini-forest of BT's microwave dishes, which didn't exactly do a huge amount for the view (although someone at BT had at least gone to the effort of putting up a sign proclaiming they'd made them as small as possible), we soon joined the ridge of the hill and a world of mighty panoramic views across a huge distance. We could see for miles and miles and miles, from the fells of the Yorkshire Dales, through to the industrial conurbation of Middlesborough. You could even just about make out ships at sea.

It was a view we'd see on and off for most of the day, with the odd interruption of forests in the morning and endless ups and downs in the afternoon.

We stopped for lunch near the obtrusive sight of a rather ugly glider club building and then stopped again a mile later for a cup of tea at Lord Stones where a cafe sits buried in the hillside.

Our guide book made it sound like some sort of burger van style place where someone called Frank would be propping up the bar with a huge cup of tea, but in reality it was a full blown cafe with draft beer and even a handpulled ale. Swifts flew over to their nests whilst chaffinches pottered around, every now and then snaffling scraps of chips off the tables.

From Lord Stones it was the beginning of the lots of ups and downs, climbing up and down hills like some sort of yo-yo. Up down, up down, up down...

Wainwright loved this bit declaring it to be "the finest section of our marathon" before adding a telling "outside Lakeland" in brackets lest anyone forget where his true loyalties lay. However for us it seemed a bit of a challenge, especially after several days of relatively flat walking. Whilst the Cleveland Way was always paved, paths were steep and a blister on the sole of my foot was throbbing slightly even if one of those odd blister plasters was on it.

Each climb seemed to be harder than the previous and we did think that by this stage we should be dancing up these hills. Yet it seemed just as hard as it always did. On comparing notes though we did console ourselves when we realised our recovery time had shrunk enormously. Rather than reaching a summit and needing half an hour collapsed on the floor to recover, I was able to just keep on going with a smile in my heart and a quick step in my feet.

I'd like to think that I'd lost some weight too but the endless fried breakfasts and pub food had probably put pay to that. (Although on arriving back home I did find out I'd lost about 2 pounds which is not to be sniffed at and just shows what an active lifestyle can do for you.)

Our final climb of the day was to the rocky crag that is home to the Wain Stones, sitting almost crown like on the hill top and as we rested, two rock climbers practised their art on the crags.

Across the flat landscape below the weather was quickly changing. The sun had long been hidden by a sweeping batch of dark clouds leaving us with a very warm and muggy day, but now the fields of golden wheat and barley below were slowly but surely being covered by dark and ominous looking clouds. As it turned out, they were the least we had to worry about and as we gingerly made our may down the now slippery cobbles that lined the path, we were ambushed by rain as we tried to get down to the main road. We had, at least, to be thankful that we'd got a good view.

* * *

Clay Bank Top is an awkward spot, a few miles from any villages. Walkers can either head east or west for shelter for the night and whilst some B&Bs will collect Coast to Coast walkers, we'd made no arrangements and faced a two and a half mile slog down the main road to get to the pub at Chop Gate (whose Norse influence means it's pronounced Chop Yat fact fans!)

Never a keen proponent of road walking, Catherine tried to navigate us by fields and stiles but instead managed to take us through nettles and brambles and after many abortive attempts to follow paths which seemed to do nothing but dump us on huge detours only to end up dumped back on the main road about a quarter of a kilometre from where we'd left it. In the end walking on the road turned out to be much faster.

We finally made it to the Buck Inn and did the now ubiquitous settling down to beer, food and a few pints amidst a clientèle made up mostly of walkers which included a mother and her 12 year old daughter whilst on the table next to us, dressed immaculately in linen pastels were two ladies who had just started the trip walking in stages and who spent the evening filling in their official "Coast to Coast Diary" whilst avoiding eating the mountain of cheese that they'd ordered.

By now we'd noticed a pub routine with most of the walkers discreetly disappearing round 9pm leaving us with the odd hard core walkers and locals who tended to sit in other parts of the bar. Having had a drink on every night of the trip, I occasionally pondered just how much I'd drunk. Whatever it was, it was a few pints, but in the end I took the decision that I needed the calories and nutrients before heading back to the bar for a top up.

Talk in the pub was, as usual, of the next days destinations and for us the remote Lion Inn beckoned - a short day which my aching legs were looking forward to most favourably.

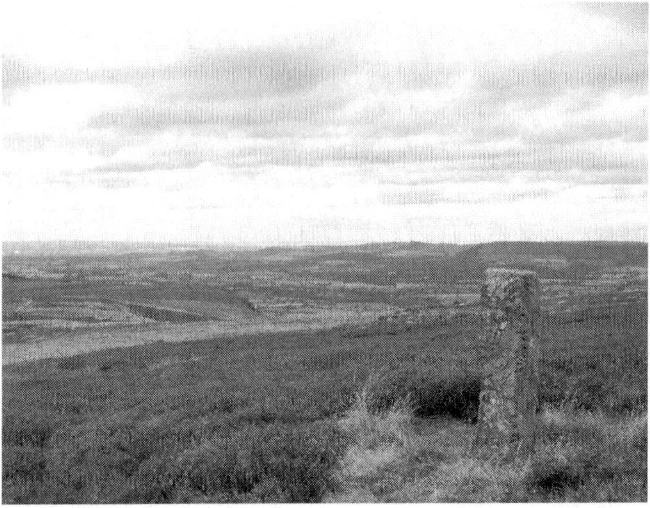

Day 12 - Clay Bank Top to Blakey Ridge

"So that was, what, day twelve? Blimey, I'm beginning to lose track..."

"So what are we going to do to allow us to move to Kirkby Stephen then?" asked Catherine.

The question came like a thunderbolt out of the blue, even more so because I was highly pre-occupied by my beard. I hadn't shaved since St Bees and by now it was getting a bit bushy. I was too busy sticking out my top lip and peering down my nose at the hairs or folding my top lip over the bottom one and feeling the brush like bristles to be thinking about some sort of new life away from London.

"Err... well... what would we do there?" I hastily replied, putting on my best "yes, I too have been contemplating huge life changing moves and not messing around with facial hair, honest guv" face.

"Well you can do your computery thing and I'll do my consultancy stuff. And we'll have a B&B too. You can write walking books and I'll write the local news round-up for the newspaper."

We'd picked up a copy of the Westmorland Gazette a few days earlier and admired how they'd filled reams of pages with Women's Institute reports and cake stall news, all compiled by some local resident who probably got paid a pound a word. Or more likely, a pound a paragraph. Yep, that kind of money would pay the bills and keep me in beer alright!

This is what walking on the North York Moors clearly does to you. It makes people think about leaving their friends behind, upping sticks, moving to Cumbria and setting up a B&B. Either that or beards.

It had been a pretty relaxing day though. We only had nine miles to do on the trail proper and once we'd done an initial climb, it was all flat and rather easy.

Although that said, we'd also had to get up to the path from the village of Chop Gate about three miles away.

Catherine was convinced there was a route we could take up to Clay Bank Top that avoided walking down the busy road we'd traversed the night before, however our maps didn't cover the area properly so everything was pretty much guesswork.

Spotting a bridleway sign near the pub she strode purposefully towards a gate in a wall proclaiming "That way!" and before I knew it, we were marching through it and up to the top corner of a field. Then we went along the top of the field. Then through a small gap in the fence that looked like it *might* be a path. Then past some decrepit huts, a few illicit stills and an abandoned caravan before finding ourselves in the far corner of an adjoining field with nowhere to go but down again to rejoin the road about 500m further along in the wrong direction.

Walking back to the pub again, we cursed the state of the local footpaths before spotting a wider and more obvious path hidden behind a builders van.

"Oh let's just stay on the road, shall we..."

Two miles and several hair raising moments on as cars hurtled far too fast round tight corners, we finally made it to the side path we'd used the previous night which would take us the remaining half mile to Clay Bank Top. The evening before we'd accidentally ended up herding a large family of grouse who didn't seem to realise that they didn't have to keep running down the road to get away from us, but that they could escape under a fence. I secretly hoped for a reprise however it was not to be.

Thankfully the subsequent walk along Urra Moor was far less "stimulating" and certainly less dangerous as we rejoined the well paved Cleveland Way for three rather flat miles of moorland walking.

Walking on the moors can sometimes be rather dull with all the views looking the same, so much so that you're never quite sure whether you're actually progressing or whether you're just going round in circles. Thankfully the North York Moors break that rule and we had several nice views down the sides to valleys and farmland below.

Bar a brief stretch of bog lasting the whole of

5m, it was never taxing and we soon arrived at Bloworth Crossing where we left the Cleveland Way and headed off on the trackbed for the Rosedale Ironstone Railway.

Constructed in 1861 it took the output of the local ironstone mines in Rosedale but was eventually closed and dismantled in 1929. At one time there was a station, staff houses and a signal box at Bloworth Crossing and it must have been a very remote posting for the staff, but now you'd be hard pressed to even know a railway was there - the only clues being the old trackbed which has since been turned into a wide and well maintained bridleway covered in cinder which was a delight underfoot. The old railway route never saw much of a gradient, leaving the walker to go through old cuttings or to stroll along large embankments.

Down below us was Farndale - a lovely peaceful dale which at one point looked set to become buried under gallons of water and converted to a reservoir which was something Wainwright decried most vocally in his veritable tome. It never happened and the farms and hamlets down below remain to this day, providing a delight to the walker to admire.

Such is the ease of this section that Wainwright himself proclaimed that "speeds will have accelerated to 5mph" and whilst Catherine wasn't going quite that fast, she did keep storming on. Well until we stopped for breaks when I got probed with Kirkby Stephen related questions anyway.

Doing a lazy loop round a hillside, we passed into another cutting before suddenly spotting our destination; The Lion Inn on Blakey Ridge.

Sat isolated in the hills, it originally served the workers of the iron mines. As the mines closed in the early 20th century trade fell so badly that the then owner, Phillip Johnson, spent most of his time farming instead. When he died his widow, and later their son, kept the business going, until the advent of the motorcar (and much later, one Alfred Wainwright) saw trade pick up once more.

Today the Lion Inn remains an old, higgledy piggledy inn with a set of rather modern and tastefully decorated B&B rooms at the back of the building.

Part of me had hoped it would turn out to be a bit like that other great isolated pub, the mighty Tan Hill Inn on the Pennine Way, a quirky little pub in the middle of nowhere on a bleak moor and where, on our visit, we found a duck sat in front of a fire and an instruction to serve ourselves as the staff were eating their tea.

The Lion Inn turned out to be a far grander enterprise, buoyed on by a greater availability of people willing to drive from miles around for a meal in the hills.

That makes it sound like a bad place but it was far from it. The food menu did look decidedly average this is true, however it was a prime example of how to do food very well. And it was also the first pub we'd visited on the trip to stock the mighty Theakston ales, and as I supped my old student favourite, Theakston XB, I dreamt of the Old Peculiar that would inevitably follow later.

Catherine on the other hand had decided on wine that night - a travesty and no mistake. Well, you just can't say no when the OP comes calling for you...

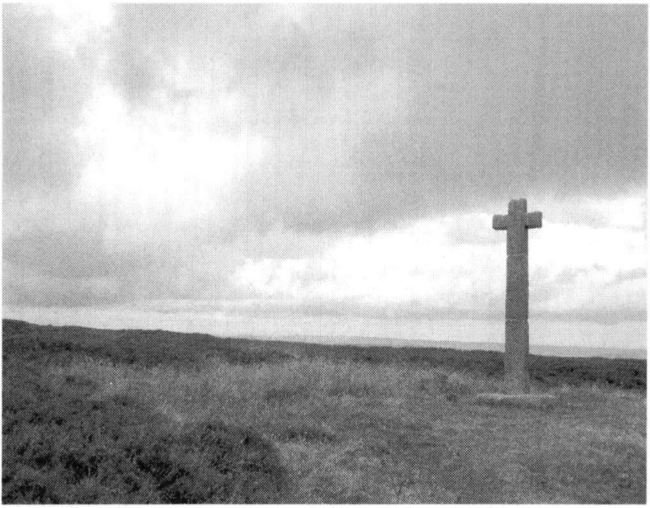

Day 13 - Blakey Ridge to Grosmont

"Well tomorrow Ernest, it's breakfast, then a bit of a walk, then we get the train and go to the beach!"

In many ways walking in Britain can be described as being just one great big pub crawl. And as you'd expect from a pub crawl, you've got the good, the bad and the ugly. And so it was on the Coast to Coast.

Well okay, maybe not the ugly. We hadn't been in any particularly awful pubs on our trip. And the bad might be pushing it a bit, but when it comes to the good, well the Coast to Coast certainly scores very highly. And when it comes to location well the Lion Inn beats them all.

The Lion Inn sits high up in the hills on a road on Blakey Ridge with next to nothing near it. Just cars, some tents and views across from miles around. After we'd eaten tea the night before, we'd popped out to get some air and saw a superb sunset in the distance. The golden sun was overlaid by low, thin clouds which were given a kind of golden halo thanks to the position of the sun.

Five minutes later we would never have seen it. Indeed I popped in for my camera and by the time I'd got back, it was almost all over. The sun had gone in; its main showing finished for the day.

And here was a packed pub whose occupants had travelled from miles around and yet most of the punters were blissfully unaware of what they'd missed. Even those who'd popped out for a quick smoke had missed the spectacle as the sunset could only be seen from the back of the building. To be able to see the best view in the area when most hadn't, made it feel even more special and I felt a sudden pang of envy at those in the tents nestled in the field alongside the pub.

That said, without doubt it's the campers who are the most extreme of the Coast to Coasters, with their large, heavy rucksacks, sore-footed shuffles and wild looks on their faces.

Usually putting in huge distances every day and starting at the crack of dawn, we rarely saw them on our own travels unless they were going in the opposite direction (and being people who go against the flow, such people were almost always camping.) But on occasions we'd see them in the pub at night, staggering around on stiff legs, talking to anyone who would listen. Most of them were solitary walkers, invariably male, who even when walking with others seemed to stay a respectful distance from their companion.

We saw one camper with a particularly wild look and perhaps the lowest slung rucksack you'd ever see. Most of it was dangling loosely below his waist; every time he stepped forward it bounced against his back. It must have been incredibly uncomfortable and certainly very bad for his back.

From the way he shuffled along, stiff legs flapping around, slowly placing one foot in front of the other, he certainly didn't seem to be enjoying himself.

Ourselves, well we seemed to be in some kind of very rare breed - staying in B&Bs or hostels yet carrying our luggage on our backs. Most walkers - and there are a substantial number in summer - do it the easy way, by making ample use of one of the several baggage transportation companies which work the route with a fleet of vans.

Just as we marvelled at the weight the campers carried on their backs, so too did others marvel at the size of our sacks. However as I pointed out to them (and to myself everytime I stared at a camper), you just get used to the weight after a few days. Lifting the rucksack on in the morning was always a chore, but once it was up, it was no bother.

Even so it was usually the campers who seemed to struggle the most although that was probably more down to their own punishing schedules and tight deadlines. If you ever hear of someone doing the Coast to Coast in eight days, they've probably camped.

But then camping is without doubt the cheapest and most flexible option. We'd booked our accommodation in early May and found many places - especially in the Lakes - declaring themselves fully booked for July already. Planning everything in advance as you need to with B&Bs in that scenario offers no flexibility; no options if things go wrong. Thankfully for us, it didn't.

* * *

With there not being huge numbers of villages and B&Bs on the trail, you find one of the potential "problems" of the Coast to Coast is that you often feel like you're setting off in some sort of convoy. So it was as we left the Lion Inn, traipsing down the roadside verge with a steady stream of walkers following behind us. Still, the shape of the hills made up for it; the required U-shaped journey along the ridge was perfect for taking in the local sights and attractions.

Well we took in the local sights. Young Ralph - an old stone cross on the hillside - is just a few hundred metres off route and provides a stunning view, but it was completely bypassed by everyone bar us and the cars which drove past it. And probably a fair few of them didn't notice. Which was a shame because it was in a lovely spot with a fine view off in the distance.

Young Ralph has an older cousin named, cunningly, Old Ralph, situated a little deeper in to the moorland, accessible by a vague and indistinct path over the heather which we couldn't really find and in the end decided not to bother with.

However in our efforts we spotted a slightly more modern piece of stonework - the bizarre sight of a small, modern looking pottery angel. On further inspection we appeared to have stumbled on some sort of "remembrance garden" littered with plaques hidden in the heather. Looking all rather hotchpotch, and presumably very unofficial it was a strange sight.

When Margery, Betty and the two Ralphs meet at night, a wedding invariably follows by all accounts. We didn't find the Margery stone - apparently a plain but ancient menhir that is supposedly extremely noticeable so perhaps it had popped off for a holiday when we tried to find it; but Fat Betty was much easier to spot.

A large rectangular stone with a circular top, Betty is given a regular coating of white paint and can be seen across the moorland for miles around.

Our guidebook proclaimed that travellers used to leave coins or food on the top of crosses like the two Ralphs and Betty in thanks for a safe journey, and over at Betty that tradition continues to this day. On her top were a smattering of pennies, a packet of mints and various biscuits, many of which were no doubt the result of a food surplus from many a Coast to Coaster's packed lunch.

And most walkers tend to end up with quite a bit. Earlier in the trip we'd ended up with quite a few apples which I'd eventually managed to get through, and now we were suffering from too many bananas, whilst a Mars bar and a Snickers sat forlorn and uneaten for several days until we chomped on them in celebration at our arrival at Keld.

* * *

Whilst not as flat and easy going as the day before, the moorland was hardly taxing and we made good progress along Danby High Moor and Glaisdale Moor with its fine views of Fryup Dale. Nothing to do with sausage and eggs, it's named after the beautiful Norse goddess Freya whilst the "up" derives from "hop" which is Ye Olde English for valley. As ever the language was corrupted over the years until it got its more artery clogging modern day name.

With Fryup Dale on the left we soon gained Glaisdale on the right and on Glaisdale we collapsed in the heather for a spot of lunch. It was an idyllic spot with just one slight problem - a contingent of agitated bees seemed to be circling the area - one so much that I got up and left it get on with whatever it seemed keen on doing.

The recipient of their anger was not us sat on a hive or anything but another bee - presumably a drone, missing half its wings and which was struggling to do anything bar saunter along the floor.

An episode of QI had once informed me that drones are often forced out of the hive by the workers towards the end of the summer season, and their wings bitten off to prevent them returning, thus ensuring the hive's precious resources are not wasted on those lazy insects and that the worker beers can survive the leaner times of autumn and winter. One could only presume this is what was happening here as we munched on our sandwiches.

* * *

We left the hills and headed to the valley floor at the village of Glaisdale where we admired its nice little train station (and felt much less well inclined towards it after spotting the sign which proclaimed there was a £1000 fine for not closing the gate - a concept which frankly sounded ridiculous) and then felt much better admiring the beautiful old packhorse Beggar's Bridge.

Now made redundant by the necessity for wider bridges which can carry heavier loads than a mule and his master, it's apparently a bit of a tourist attraction in the village, a fact one couple canoodling under it seemed blissfully unaware of until I turned up and pointed my camera in their vague direction; they quickly disentangled themselves whilst I attempted to look nonchalant from a distance.

Perturbing people over, we headed for a brief stint in East Arnecliff Wood with its mediaeval stone flagged path (laid centuries ago for the pannier ponies which once walked along the route taking goods between villages) and as this ended we heard the age old woodland sound of a loud, mechanical "hmmmmmmmmm"

Emerging on to yet another road (this section having suffered greatly from the old tarmacadam) we found a road sweeper moving barely at walking speed along the otherwise quiet country lane. We followed it all the way to the village of Egton Bridge where we finally lost its company, thus allowing us to pull the cotton wool out of our ears once more.

We passing a lovely looking country pub,

festooned with hanging baskets and positively glowing in the sun that had finally poked its head out through the cloud. It was hard to resist its charms but somehow we managed it and made our way to the stepping stones and the track to Grosmont.

We had a slight hurry in our step, and the reason was waiting for us there. At the heart of the village sits a level crossing and two train stations, sited side by side.

One - a single platform sparsely decorated and even more sparsely populated was the mainline railway platform for services to Whitby and Middlesborough. The other was the far grander looking home of the North York Moors Railway, a steam railway which was doing a roaring trade with its engines in full flow.

Heritage railways are wonderful things and it is naturally compulsory to stand on the platforms with huge grins as the smoke of the engine fills the air, and that had been good enough reason as any for us to hurry along earlier in the day. We'd arrived with just enough time to catch the 4:30 bound for Pickering although we wouldn't be able to do the full route. Instead we'd have to change at the penultimate stop of Levisham in order to catch the last train back to Grosmont, but it was good enough for me and the trip through the forests and moorland was well worth it.

Our outbound train had been packed to the rafters but our return was far quieter and being at the front of the train I naturally spent much of the journey sticking my head out of the window as soot hit my face and filled my hair - which I'd be finding for weeks after.

It was not until we arrived back at Grosmont that we found out that the rest of the passengers had turned their noses up at our relatively modern carriage and had instead been enjoying the polished wood of some rather old LNER carriages, whilst the end of the train was a plush "first class" viewing carriage with an armchair looking out on the rails. Could there be a finer way to travel? Surely not.

I longed to spend more time on the line, popping on and off, exploring the stations and the land around them. The steam trains also make regular trips down the mainline to Whitby which must be a fantastic way to arrive at the seaside. Sadly we didn't have the time - a real shame but without a day to spare, we'd never have been able to do it justice.

* * *

With the steam railway and its huge wooden level crossing gates at the heart of the village, Grosmont seemed like a village stuck in a timewarp, helped by having its own proper old fashioned Co-op. Local teenagers - girls as well as boys - wandered around happily in overalls and NYMR high visibility vests, whilst train drivers drove their engines with huge grins on their faces.

Even our B&B acted the part, decked out in an almost Victorian style with old flowered wallpaper and brass taps; a grandfather clock standing tall and proud in the hallway.

It was a difficult place to leave the next morning, even more so by the huge steep climb up the hill out of the village and the fact that the railway seemed to decide to do some major steam train shunting just as we wanted to leave, resulting in us being stranded on the wrong side of the level crossing... Yeah, I'm sure we could have made it across somehow... But hey, sometimes you've just got to stand around and watch trains... Hoot hoot...

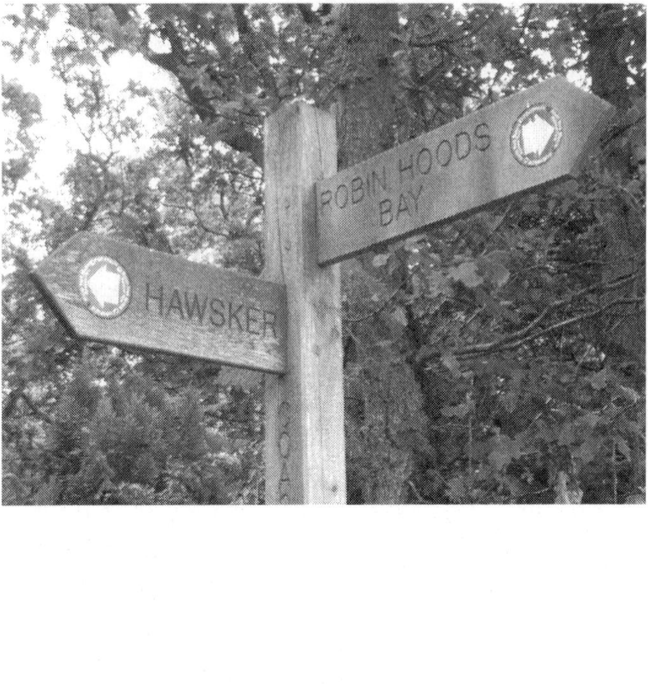
ROBIN HOODS
BAY
HAWSKER

Day 14 - Grosmont to Robin Hood's Bay

"I feel like I don't want to stop. That I just want to keep on walking..."

"Are you doing the Coast to Coast then?" asked the man behind the Post Office counter at the Grosmont Co-operative Stores. Given the size of the rucksack sat on my back, it was a pretty safe assumption.

"Second most popular trail in the world," he went on. "Second only to that Andes trail. More popular than New Zealand. We get people from all over the world doing it. Even from Taiwan!"

He seemed stunned that people would come all the way from the other side of the world to get soaked and cold in the hills of Northern England. And to be rather frank, so was I.

"Really?" I replied. "Because almost everyone I've seen seems to have come from the North of England!"

It was perhaps a slight exaggeration however there was an element of truth in it. We really had seen a large number of Northerners whilst we'd been out walking.

The popularity of a walk like the Coast to Coast is such that, inevitably, you regularly see the same group of people. Your itineraries may be slightly different however if you're all doing the same route in the same number of days, well you're going to keep on bumping in to people. Often I'd play a game and see if I could correctly guess who we would be sharing the breakfast table with the next morning.

However it was soon to end. It was our fourteenth and final day; the day we'd finally complete our journey from west to east and arrive in Robin Hood's Bay.

And it being the last day, we began to see lots of people who we didn't recognise - the people who had done the route in 12 days, 13 days, hey, maybe even 9. The ones who had caught up with us, and those who were going even slower, had taken a rest day or whatever.

The climb out of Grosmont was spent following two such people - a Sloane Ranger-esque couple, where the woman had an amazingly small rucksack with a large bum-bag underneath it. As she walked, the two bags moved in different ways and the whole effect was as if an ant had stood on its hind legs and was walking up the road.

Without the burden of weight that we had, they soon sped on ahead as we hit the moorland, helped by us wandering over the heather filled land seeking a pair of stone circles which barely seemed the effort once we did locate them, and admiring the local wildlife which to seemed to consist mostly of sheep and ants.

Ah the wildlife. Inevitably going over such huge

distances meant you are going to see a lot although much of the animals I could tick off in my I-Spy book seemed to consist of different kinds of sheep. Every now and then Catherine would proclaim something like "Is that a peregrine falcon?" but almost without fail it would turn out to be a crow or a blackbird.

Swifts and swallows were plentiful, grouse even more so whilst in several fields butterflies had danced happily around our heads. A turkey once wandered out on to the road. However we never did see what is apparently an amazing sight.

Our guide book proclaimed we may see "the horrendous sight of a stoat dancing before a terrified, hypnotised rabbit" but most of the fluffy creatures we saw were running in an un-hypnotised fashion across fields, or lying in the middle of the road rather squashed. I did see a mole and a hedgehog however both were similarly lifeless.

Coming off the moorland we entered Little Beck Wood where a sign proclaimed we may see roe deer or foxes, and although initially peaceful and rather tranquil we saw little bar fellow walkers.

Then came a sudden change in the woodland life - people, lots of people, ambling around in trainers, shrieking kids running around.

We were suddenly back in civilisation, near a pretty waterfall complete with busy tea shop, and equipped with two huffing and rather rotund men hogging the best view of the cascade by parking their similarly large cameras on tripods there. Even seeing me struggle to actually take a photograph due to their piles of equipment getting in the way did nothing for their selfish hearts and their tripods remained unbudged.

After nearly two weeks spent with lovely, friendly and kind people, it was a harsh welcome back to the real world of selfish, self-centred and ignorant people and I just wanted to pick up their tripods and throw them in to the waterfall below.

Quite what they even expected to catch on the cameras by setting them up so perfectly was beyond me. Were they expecting some rare woodland nymph to suddenly pop out, see the crowds and then hurry away as fast as possible?

Walking through the rest of the woods was similarly disheartening – the kids barging all over the paths; the woman who had barely walked five minutes from her car but couldn't cope without lighting up a cigarette – and sadly I couldn't wait to be out of such a lovely place. The empty moorland afterwards was far more inviting and welcoming, back amongst our "own kind" once more. But it was a sharp reminder that soon we'd be back in the normal world properly. The walk would not last forever, even more notable as the moorland fell away once more and left us in areas filled with holiday parks and caravan sites.

The Coast To Coast took us through one such park before finally hitting the coastline. We'd been welcomed by a staff member who had told us to feel free to use the toilets, however that good vibe was spoiled by an unfriendly and downright patronising sign demanding we "respect the privacy of our residents" by not looking through the caravan windows.

It was a ridiculous request. No one feels the need to put such a sign at the entrance to a housing estate. "Waterfield Avenue is a residential area. Please don't gawp through the net curtains of number 42". If such a sign really needed to be erected - and that's dubious - it could have been worded in a much warmer way rather leaving a bitter taste in the mouth of walkers.

Still we were heading for the sea and that was enough to put some joy in our hearts. For most of the afternoon Whitby had been in our sights and if you hadn't known, you would have assumed it was the place that the Coast to Coast ended. But instead Wainwright had a trick up his sleeve and we were heading south, rejoining once more the Cleveland Way for the last stretch to Robin Hood's Bay.

The cliff path that would take us there was decked out with a plethora of wild flowers making it a lovely stroll, joined by a number of day trippers taking the path down from Whitby.

Our destination remained hidden until right near the end and even when the bay itself appeared, the town remained invisible for some time. Then, in a crack in the bushes, as if by magic, it appeared; the old buildings of the town suddenly visible next to the sea.

Coming in through the grand streets lined with Victorian guest houses, we made our way steadily towards the beach, fighting our way through the crowds to finally arrive at the Bay Hotel and the sea beyond.

It was hopelessly busy and the journey of two walkers with giant rucksacks meant little here, but we'd made it. Enthusiastically dipping our boots in the sea, we left our pebbles splashing around in the waves as we adjourned to the pub to celebrate our completion with our fellow walkers.

It seemed an appropriate way to end. Usually such long distance paths end at some dull location like a roundabout or a shopping arcade, with no one around to revel in the occasion with you. You're just some nutter in scruffy clothes with walking poles and a lump of cloth on your back. But here, others knew too. Others to compare notes and mutter things like "wasn't the Lakes awful?" or discuss the purchasing of celebratory certificates and plaques.

However that wasn't our only celebration. We'd found a special treat to round off our trip.

At Grosmont Catherine had spied a poster proclaiming, entirely by coincidence, that folk music legends the Waterson Family would be preforming at Old St Stephen's Church in the village that very night.

As soon as we'd arrived at Robin Hood's Bay we got tickets and after a hasty meal at the chip shop and a quick shower we headed right to the top of the village and beyond to visit the old church to see and hear the vocal stylings of some legends of the folk world. Eliza and Martin Carthy were otherwise engaged, however Mike and Norma Waterson and a plethora of talented family members (and someone called Jill) more than made up for it in a concert in the now defunct church which normally sits quietly at the top of the hill with little around it.

As the sun went in, we headed back to the bay for another celebratory pint of two - to sit down and relax.

The following morning would see us heading home. It would all be over. The thought of going back to work in an office in West London just didn't appeal. We'd spent fourteen days walking across some of the finest landscape in Britain and I'd loved it.

Except the Lakes. Cos frankly they were awful.

THE END
COAST TO COAST WALK
ALTITUDES
ST BEES TO ROBIN HOODS BA
192 MILES

About The Author

Andrew Bowden was born and raised in Hyde, Greater Manchester and spent much of his early years being dragged around Etherow Country Park a few miles from his parents' house.

After abandoning hiking in his teenage years in favour of spending far too much time in front of computer games, he returned to the hills after falling in love with a section of the Pennine Way.

Since rediscovering his hiking boots, he has walked a fair number of long distance trails, including the Coast to Coast, Pennine Way, West Highland Way and the Cumbria Way.

He writes about walking on his website, Rambling Man, at *http://ramblingman.org.uk/*, and can also be found on Twitter at *http://twitter.com/andrewbowden*

Andrew lives in London with his partner Catherine and son, Sam.

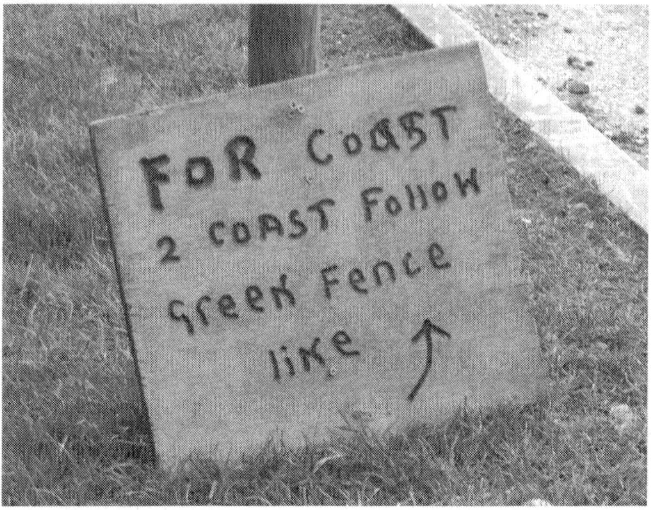
FOR COAST
2 COAST Follow
Green Fence
like

Planning Your Own Trip Walking the Coast to Coast

If you've got this far, there's a possibility that you've been inspired to walk it yourself. Either that or you've watched that Julia Bradbury do it on the telly and thought "that looks great!"

Whichever way you've come to the Coast to Coast doesn't matter. What matters is that you've thought "Yes, I could do that! Sign me up! How do I do it then?" You have, haven't you?

You have? Great! So what do you need to know to plan your trip walking from one side of the west of England, to the east?

What is the walk like?

It has been on TV and was created by a walking superstar, so the Coast to Coast is quite a famous route. And it's popular. And that means people sometimes think it's going to be easy - like walking in the park.

It's not. It's 190 miles long, and there are some difficult bits, especially in the Lake District. And if the weather is bad, well it can be very difficult indeed. And I'm saying that as an experienced walker who has been up to his knees in bog on the Pennine Way.

I don't want to put people off doing the Coast to Coast, because it's a very rewarding route and in many parts it's nice and easy going. I've heard of those who in their 70s and 80s who have done it. So if you've done some hill walking you should be fine.

However do not underestimate the Coast to Coast. To do it successfully you will need to be fit, have good walking boots and be very competent with a map and compass. Preferably you'll have done some long distance walking before too.

That said, what should you expect? Well the Coast to Coast is an amazingly varied route, and no two days are the same. There are fells, moorland, fields and mining history. In creating the walk Wainwright really went out to make it interesting. It really does seem to cover everything you could ever possibly want in a long distance walk.

The Coast to Coast is 190 miles/306km long in distance.

Planning an itinerary

Unless you're camping, you need to work out your itinerary in advance and get it booked. As the Coast to Coast goes through many small villages, and is a very popular route, accommodation is very limited and booked up early.

The Coast to Coast could be walked all year round, however navigation and conditions can be difficult in poor conditions. As such, it is best walked in the period of May to October.

There are a couple of different possible itineraries and I have listed three: 12 days, 14 days and 15 days. Based on my experience I recommend the 15 day one. The 12 day version includes some very long distances and is recommended only for fit and experienced walkers.

The towns and villages listed in the itinerary below have been selected as they all have facilities - every one has a pub, and most have shops too. Where there are no shops, pubs and B&Bs will be able to provide packed lunches.

12 Day Itinerary
- Day 1: St Bees to Ennerdale Bridge (14 miles, 22½km)
- Day 2: Ennerdale Bridge to Rosthwaite (14 miles, 22½km)
- Day 3: Rosthwaite to Patterdale (17 miles, 27¼km)
- Day 4: Patterdale to Shap (15 miles, 24km)
- Day 5: Shap to Kirkby Stephen (20 miles, 32km)
- Day 6: Kirkby Stephen to Keld (11 miles, 17¾km)
- Day 7: Keld to Reeth (10½ miles, 17km)
- Day 8: Reeth to Richmond (15 miles, 24km)
- Day 9: Richmond to Ingleby Arncliffe (23 miles, 37km)
- Day 10: Ingleby Arncliffe to Clay Bank Top (11 miles, 17¾km)
- Day 11: Clay Bank Top to Glaisdale (18 miles, 29km)
- Day 12: Glaisdale to Robin Hood's Bay (19 miles, 30½km)

14 Day Itinerary
- Day 1: St Bees to Ennerdale Bridge (14 miles, 22½km)
- Day 2: Ennerdale Bridge to Rosthwaite (14 miles, 22½km)
- Day 3: Rosthwaite to Patterdale (17 miles, 27¼km)
- Day 4: Patterdale to Bampton (11½ miles, 18½km)
- Day 5: Bampton to Orton (11½ miles, 18½km)
- Day 6: Orton to Kirby Stephen (12½ miles, 20km)
- Day 7: Kirkby Stephen to Keld (11 miles, 17¾km)
- Day 8: Keld to Reeth (10½ miles, 17km)
- Day 9: Reeth to Richmond (15 miles, 24km)
- Day 10: Richmond to Ingleby Arncliffe (23 miles, 37km)
- Day 11: Ingleby Arncliffe to Clay Bank Top (11 miles, 17¾km)
- Day 12: Clay Bank Top to The Lion Inn (9 miles, 14½km)
- Day 13: The Lion Inn to Grosmont (12½ miles, 20km)
- Day 14: Grosmont to Robin Hood's Bay (15½miles, 25km)

15 Day Itinerary
- Day 1: St Bees to Ennerdale Bridge (14 miles, 22½km)
- Day 2: Ennerdale Bridge to Rosthwaite (14

miles, 22½km)
- Day 3: Rosthwaite to Grasmere (9 miles, 14½km)
- Day 4: Grasmere to Patterdale (8 miles, 13¼km)
- Day 5: Patterdale to Bampton (11½ miles, 18½km)
- Day 6: Bampton to Orton (11½ miles, 18½km)
- Day 7: Orton to Kirby Stephen (12½ miles, 20km)
- Day 8: Kirkby Stephen to Keld (11 miles, 17¾km)
- Day 9: Keld to Reeth (10½ miles, 17km)
- Day 10: Reeth to Richmond (15 miles, 24km)
- Day 11: Richmond to Ingleby Arncliffe (23 miles, 37km)
- Day 12: Ingleby Arncliffe to Clay Bank Top (11 miles, 17¾km)
- Day 13: Clay Bank Top to The Lion Inn (9 miles, 14½km)
- Day 14: The Lion Inn to Grosmont (12½ miles, 20km)
- Day 15: Grosmont to Robin Hood's Bay (15½miles, 25km)

A Note on Walking Richmond to Ingleby Arncliffe

As a big town, Richmond is an obvious place to stay overnight. However doing so means a 23 mile slog the next day. It's doable but hard going. However there is a way to avoid it.

The answer is to keep on walking when you get to Richmond. Carry on for 4½ miles to Brompton-on-Swale. Then either stay overnight in Brompton or catch the regular bus to Richmond and return on it the next morning. The next day you will be seriously thankful you did.

Breaking the walk up for several trips

If you haven't got time to do it all in one go, you can break the Coast to Coast up in a few ways.

The most sensible place to split the route is half way at Kirkby Stephen, which is on the Settle to Carlisle railway link.

Alternatively you can do it into three sections by breaking at Shap and Richmond. Neither have a railway station, however local bus routes connect both with railway stations. Buses run from Shap to Penrith, and from Richmond to Darlington, both of which are served by mainline services.

Due to limited public transport services on other parts of the trail, there are no other easy ways to split the Coast to Coast up.

Rest Days

Walking 12-15 days consecutively may sound a lot, although if you keep your daily mileage reasonable, you'll find it easier than you may think. However you may want to plan in some places where you can have a day off.

If you're going to take a day off hiking, then you might as well do it at a place where there's plenty to do. The following suggestions are all worth considering:

Grasmere - very early in the Coast to Coast, however Grasmere is a walker's paradise and a lovely village to boot. You can potter around the shops, stroll in the nearby hills or maybe buy some of Grasmere's famous gingerbread.

Kirkby Stephen - almost half way through your trip, this little town is in the beautiful Eden Valley, and is on the Settle to Carlisle line if you fancy a trip on an iconic train line. There's also a bike hire shop and craft shops to explore.

Richmond - the largest town on the Coast to Coast, Richmond is a bustling place with a castle and lots of history to explore. It's an ideal candidate to rest before pushing on for a very long day the next day. However after all that walking in the relative piece and quiet, this can be a rather disorientating place and even though we only stopped there for less than an hour, I personally couldn't wait to get out!

Grosmont - with only a few miles left to Robin Hood's Bay, Grosmont might seem a bonkers place to stop. However Grosmont is home to the North York Moors Railway, which means steam trains! It's a lovely little line with lots of places to potter around and get off and walk through moorland and forest. Seriously recommended, but do - of course - check the railway is running on your visit! Trains operate daily in the summer school holidays, however at other times operating patterns vary.

Finding and booking accommodation

The Coast to Coast is very busy and in the Lake District in particular, it can be very hard to find accommodation. Advance booking is pretty much essential if you're walking in the summer.

Doreen Whitehead has been publishing an accommodation guide for the route for over 15 years and it is updated annually, and a print copy is available for £5. A free online version is also available. Details of both can be found at *http://www.coasttocoastguides.co.uk/*.

Whilst Doreen's guide provides excellent coverage, it is not exhaustive and you may need to search online for alternatives.

Hostels and bunkhouses

With one exception, all the hostels on the Coast to Coast sit firmly in the Lake District. The hostels on or near the route are:

YHA Ennerdale - note that this is a few miles beyond from Ennerdale Bridge.

YHA Black Sail - iconic remote hostel four miles on from YHA Ennerdale.

YHA Honister Hause - about three miles before Rosthwaite.

YHA Borrowdale - just outside Rosthwaite.

YHA Grasmere Butharlyp Howe - YHA hostel in the village.

Thorney How Independent Hostel, Grasmere - former YHA hostel on the edges of the village.

YHA Patterdale

Kirkby Stephen Hostel (formerly YHA Kirkby Stephen, now independent)

Camping

Many people who walk the Coast to Coast do so with a tent and the trail is very well served for campers. There are some campsites, but many pubs and farms offer space for walkers to pitch up and there's a few camping barns too. Doreen's accommodation guide (noted above) includes information on camping.

There's no legal right to wild camp in England, although it is tolerated in some areas, especially in the Lake District, which has a plethora of excellent wild camping spots. However unless you're an experienced wild camper, we'd recommend staying on proper facilities.

Getting to/from the Coast to Coast

Because the route takes you from one side of the UK to the other, the most sensible way to arrive and depart is by public transport. St Bees in Cumbria is on the Cumbrian Coast Line, which is a bit slow although rather nice - trains run from Carlisle or Lancaster - the route Lancaster route is, I'm told, the most scenic. Both Carlisle and Lancaster have excellent rail links with the rest of the country.

Robin Hood's Bay no longer has a railway station, however there are buses to Whitby or Scarborough. Whitby is nearer although there are more trains from Scarborough and the bus journey is not much longer. Scarborough trains go via York, which also has excellent rail links.

Guide Books and Maps

The popularity of the Coast to Coast means that there's a huge number of guide books, in several languages. The following are our recommendations.

The obvious book to mention when talking about the Coast to Coast is the original *A Coast To Coast Walk: A Pictorial Guide* by Wainwright himself. It's the book that started it all off and we carried a copy with us at all times. It's full of history and information as well as detail of the route, set out in Wainwright's handwritten style complete with his line drawings and occasional doodles. The Second Edition of the book was updated by Chris Jesty, and published in 2010.

Although Wainwright wrote his pictorial guide in such a way that you can navigate using it, you'll probably want to plot your route out on a map as well. We tended to use Wainwright in the evenings to see what we'd done, and it does make a great memento of the trip.

Most people prefer to use a more modern guide book for day to day navigating and the popularity of the route means that there are many.

Based on previous experience we recommend Aurum Press's *The Coast to Coast Walk (Recreational Path Guide)* by Martin Wainwright (who is no relation).

The Aurum guides are clear and interesting reads, and always include Ordnance Survey 1:25,000 scale mapping. They also show a good area around the route, just in case you get lost.

If you prefer just to use maps, then there are two options. Firstly, there is the *A-Z Adventure Series Coast to Coast Map* book. The excellent A-Z Adventure Series includes Ordnance Survey mapping for the whole route (at the 1:25,000 Explorer scale), as well as an index to help you find places. The book is a similar size to a map and will fit neatly in a map case, and is a lot easier to fold in wind! It has a small, compact size.

Alternatively you might want to consider Harvey's two maps of the route. These are traditional paper maps, with Harvey's own mapping at a scale of 1:40,000, so are less detailed than the A-Z maps.

Finally, if you'd prefer to take a stack of Ordnance Survey maps with you (and it will be quite a stack), you will need the following:

Landranger (1:50,000) - 89, 90, 91, 92. 93, 94, 99

Explorer (1:25,000) - OL4, OL5, OL19, OL26, OL27, OL30, 302, 303, 304

Know how to use a map and a compass

As the Coast to Coast is a completely unofficial route, waymarking is variable. The Wainwright Society has waymarked much of the route, and some community groups and individuals have placed their own signs to help the walkers. However the Coast to Coast is not a trail that you can navigate using just waymarks alone.

As such you will need a guide book with good

quality maps in it (such as the Aurum guide book detailed above), or you will need maps. You'll also need to know how to use a compass.

The importance of this cannot be underestimated. Whilst we were walking the Coast to Coast we saw some people who were woefully unprepared. Don't be the man we saw who was navigating through the Lakes with a laminated A5 card that showed next to nothing other than a wiggly line with some place names. Had there not been other people around, chances are that he would have got very lost. There's not a year that goes by when local mountain rescue teams don't have to rescue lost Coast to Coast walkers.

Make sure you have a good map and compass, and know how to use them. So if you, or one of your party doesn't know how to use a map and compass together, I'd learn. Better still, make sure everyone in the party knows. You will need those skills.

Knowing how to use a map and compass together will really help you and will (hopefully!) stop you getting lost. And if you do get lost, you'll stand a chance of finding your way again.

And finally, and any questions

Hopefully now you're now raring at the bit ready to go so there's little to do other than offer you some sage advice. Take some good, comfortable, well broken in boots and some good breathable waterproofs - it's often wet in the Lake District especially.

And where it's wet, wet boots inevitably follow. A

tip, which many walkers don't seem to know about boots wet inside is when you take them off, fill them with balls of newspaper. The newspaper soaks up the water from inside the boot, thus drying them out. It works a lot faster than letting them air dry. Try checking and replacing the newspaper after a few hours to help.

On a related wetness note, if there's one thing you should pack, it's waterproofing wax for your boots. Waterproofing on hiking boots does wear off (something people often don't realise) and we had problems with boots getting soaked inside because of it even though both pairs were relatively new (that said, they had gone in many bogs and things...)

At the outdoor shop at Kirkby Stephen the owner recommended Nikwax Waterproofing Wax for Leather. From experience it works very well, and you can apply it even to soaked boots. I tend to slap it on every few days just to make sure - it does work, and maintains the boot's breathability if the boot is lined with something like Gore-Tex. If you don't have leather boots, consult your local outdoor shop as similar products exist for other boot types.

Still it doesn't always rain. Take your suncream and insect bite cream as well and you'll be covered for all occasions! And don't hesitate to ask any questions via my website at *http://ramblingman.org.uk/*. You will also find a regularly updated copy of this guide there.

Discover other books by Andrew Bowden

Find out more about these titles at *http://ramblingman.org.uk/books*:

- Doing the Dales Way
- The Secret Coast to Coast
- Walking with the Last Prince
- See You In Kirk Yetholm
- Rambling Man Walks The Ridgeway
- Rambling Man Walks The North Downs Way
- Rambling Man Walks the East Highland Way

Connect with Andrew Bowden

Visit the Rambling Man website:
http://ramblingman.org.uk

Follow on Twitter:
http://twitter.com/ramblingmanuk

Find on Facebook:
http://www.facebook.com/pages/Rambling-Man/253196934720776

Watch on YouTube:
http://www.youtube.com/user/ramblingmanorguk

Made in the USA
San Bernardino, CA
19 February 2017